CONCILIUM

CONCILIUM
ADVISORY COMMITTEE

CONCILIUM 2019/3

Technology:
Between Apocalypse and Integration

Edited by

Linda Hogan, Michelle Becka, João Vila-Chã

SCM Press · London

Published in 2019 by SCM Press, 3rd Floor, Invicta House, 108–114 Golden Lane, London EC1Y 0TG.

SCM Press is an imprint of Hymns Ancient & Modern Ltd (a registered charity) 13A Hellesdon Park Road, Norwich NR6 5DR, UK

www.concilium.in

ISBN 978-0-334-03154-3

Printed in the UK by
Ashford, Hampshire

Concilium is published in March, June, August, October, December

Contents

Part Four: Theological Forum

Contributors   144

Editorial

Between Apocalypse and Integration

The ubiquity and convergence of technologies, together with the speed of their development means that many of us are unaware of the depth of their impact and of the philosophical and societal challenges that they may pose. Some commentators warn of a dystopian future, with the displacement of humans by superintelligences and deepening polarisation and inequality. Others anticipate a future of greater wealth and opportunity and of significant scientific advances. It is vital therefore that, as technological development breaches a new threshold, that its meaning, significance and impact is considered. This will require multi-disciplinary forms of reflection since the challenges and opportunities posed by technology affect all aspects of human life.

Of course, human beings have long-since grappled with the nature and significance of technology, and its implications for our understanding of our place in the world, so these questions are now not entirely new.[1] Indeed, reflection on the nature of this relationship has been a consistent feature of Christian thought.[2] Christians through the ages have pursued advancements in technology in the belief that increasing human knowledge is a noble calling, while many of the most influential scientists and technologists drew their inspiration and rationale from their Christian world-views.[3] However, as Jacques Ellul has argued, recent decades have seen a sea-change, so that the fascination with technology which had been grounded in the Christian world-view, has been reordered and now risks no longer being at the service of humanity. Moreover, it is arguable that recent technological developments have brought us to the frontiers of human understanding, so that questions of human nature, theological and philosophical anthropology, as well as of human futures and eschatology are now raised in ways that heretofore were not in play.

The ethical and political dimensions of the technological revolution have also become matters of public concern. In every age ethics has had to grapple with the upper limits of technology. Today the focus is on artificial intelligence, gene editing and big data. However, citizens are concerned about their abilities to deliberate and decide on these issues when our knowledge is constantly being outstripped by advancements in technology. They are also concerned about the values and priorities that set the course for technological developments – that is, which issues are regarded as urgent, and who decides. Can one speak any more about the obligating features of being human when technological developments have the potential to impact human identity and personhood so profoundly? Will the future of work undergo a fundamental revolution similar to that of the 18th and 19th centuries? How can citizens influence the future shape of society when the capacity for technological innovation is overwhelmingly in private ownership? The ethical and political questions being raised by technology are not just about the future of science, they are also fundamentally about the kind of society we want, and the values by which we want to live.

This issue of *Concilium* seeks to explore the multi-faceted dimensions of technological advancements through a philosophical and theological lens and considers a range of inter-related themes. This volume opens with an essay by Paul Dumouchel entitled *The Impacts of Technology: Anthropological Foundations*. Dumouchel probes the question of how technology is to be understood in its relation to human beings and their activities. This foundational question has been asked and answered in different historical periods, and in his reflections Dumouchel highlights the implications of Hegel's framing of, and response to this question, particularly for the western theological and political imaginary. Dumouchel is critical of analyses that externalise technology and that treat it as an invention that is distinct and separate from human activity. Rather, technology ought to be conceptualised as a form of human activity, not as artefact or product. He draws on Gibson's notion of affordances to argue that technologies can be understood as 'the various activities through which humans domesticate and materialize affordances' thus repositioning the human relation to technology. Moreover, he argues that this reframing has implications, not only for how we understand ourselves as a species, but also for the ways in which the ethical and political dimensions of technology are appraised. Indeed, Dumouchel is highly critical of ethical analyses that see the issues through the lens of the individual user, and he argues for a more comprehensive analysis in which the political and the ethical dimensions of this aspect of human activity is appraised. Where Dumouchel considers the human relation to technology, broadly considered, and how this can be conceptualised, Benedikt Göcke focuses specifically on very recent developments in artificial intelligence and synthetic biology. Göcke discusses the innovative nature of recent technological developments, stressing the opportunities and challenges that are afforded to human society through machine learning and deep learning. He highlights in particular how this recursive capacity of machines to learn, represents a significant milestone in technological development, one that is and will continue to impact on human life in fundamental ways. Thus, argues Göcke, forms of artificial intelligence and of synthetic biology require us not only to reflect on the opportunities and risks of these technologies, but they also prompt a reappraisal of our concept of the human being, and of human life itself.

Continuing this theme, but through a more explicitly theological lens is Paolo Benanti's *Artificial Intelligence, Robots, Bio-engineering and Cyborgs: New Theological Challenges?* suggests that recent technological advances raise not only questions about new artefacts and their uses, but rather raise profound questions about human beings and our place in the world. Moreover, in Benanti's estimation these questions require a theological positioning and response, since they ultimately pose questions about the human vocation as beings-in-the-world. However, Benanti is also insistent that, although theological contributions to these foundational questions are essential, they must be complemented by reflections from other fields of expertise, since these new frontiers of knowledge highlight the importance of, and need for, interdisciplinary studies, as never before. While Benanti reflects on the theological meanings and possibilities of new technological advances, Dominik Burkard takes a historical perspective and asks the question whether there has been a particular hostility to technology in the history of the Catholic Church. His answer is that there have been different responses at different times, and that, even in periods that are often assumed to be hostile to technology, as for example the Inquisition, recent research presents a differentiated and sometimes surprising picture. Indeed as the essays in this volume suggest, motifs of both apocalypse and integration are already present in the tradition.

In the opening essay of this volume Paul Dumouchel highlights how, in different historical periods, the relationship between humans and their technologies is framed in different ways, often yielding very different results. The western framing of the technology question is problematized by both Peter Kanyandago and Kuruvilla Pandikattu. Kanyandago analyses the persistence of colonialism in modern technological discourse and development. Considered from an African perspective Kanyandago argues that in ways similar to the manner in which African culture has been marginalised, so too have African technologies been marginalised and undervalued. Moreover, he argues, this happened from the very early colonial engagements with Africa. His essay is a plea for alternative form of discourse in which the history of Africa's technological capacity is properly appreciated. This, he suggests, can be part of a process by which the humanity and dignity of the African comes to be respected and rehabilitated as it should. Kuruvilla Pandikattu brings perspectives from India to the discussion about technology and its limits and possibilities. He draws on a diverse range of sources, from the philosophical and theological to the literary, proposing an 'Indian way' of approaching the current technological and cultural revolution. He argues that the 'Indian way' brings a philosophical and spiritual perspective to bear on technology, thus allowing for an approach to these transformations that puts human flourishing at its core.

The question of human flourishing is central to Sharon Bong's essay on *Technology in the Service of Humanity: Perspectives on Gender and Inclusion*. Bong's feminist lens on technology and its significance allows some fundamental questions about how we understand our place in the world to be raised. Deploying the motif of the womb as a site of exploration, Bong asks readers to consider the question of human relationships both to humans and other animals and to the environment in two distinct modes, first, through the centring of the human in creation based on *Laudato Si'*; and second with, the decentring of the human in creation through

10

reproductive technologies. Janina Loh takes up these ethical questions particularly by focussing on how new technologies, especially virtuality, have the capacity to change concepts of responsibility. In view of the complexities of the ethical challenges of new technologies Loh insists that the category of individual responsibility is insufficient. Rather collective responsibility and networks of responsibility need also to the deployed in the service of humane and inclusive technological development.

Our reflections on technology end with an essay by Jacob Erikson who places technology in its planetary and theological context. He revisits the technological dimensions of Lynn White's celebrated reflections on the roots of our ecological crisis and, with White as a spring-board, he repositions human technoculture and digital material as vibrant matter animate in political ecologies, and as situated in the context of deep planetary geophysical time. He ends with a proposition that considers how the concepts of 'planetary solidarity' and 'moral pleasure' in theology might help orient our path through the twin perils of environmental despair and false hope in technology.

The Theological Forum contributions are diverse and capture some of the interesting recent happenings in theology. The Forum features two reflections on the current shape of theology, both of which were presented in March 2018 at the inaugural meeting of the European Academy of Religion in Bologna, Italy. In the first Enrico Galavotti reflects on theology from Vatican II, while in the second Leonardo Paris discusses doing theology in Italy today. Also included in the Forum is an insightful comment on the praxis of faith consistent investing by Seamus Finn who is responsible for the Faith Consistent Investing programme for the Oblate Investment Pastoral Trust. Our volume ends with Jon Sobrino's moving tribute to Archbishop Oscar Romero.

Linda Hogan, Michelle Becka, João Vila-Chã

Notes

1. Cf. Jacques Ellul, *La technique: ou, L'en jeu du siècle, Collection Sciences politiques* (Paris: A. Colin, 1954); Jacques Ellul, *The Technological Society*, Vintage Book (New York: Vintage Books, 1964).

2. Cf. Jacques Ellul, *L'empire du non-sens: l'art et la société technicienne*, 1. éd, La Politique éclatée (Paris: Presses universitaires de France, 1980); Jacques Ellul, *The Technological System* (New York: Continuum, 1980); Jacques Ellul, La subversion du christianisme, Empreintes (Paris: Seuil, 1984).

Cf. Ugo Baldini et al., Catholic Church and Modern Science: Documents from the Archives of the Roman Congregations of the Holy Office and the Index, Fontes Archivi Sancti Officii Romani (Roma: Libreria editrice vaticana, 2009).

Part One: Technology: Foundational Questions

The Impacts of Technology: Anthropological Foundations

PAUL DUMOUCHEL

This article argues that technological activity constitutes a fundamental part of who we humans are as a species. Therefore the impacts of technology on the natural and social world should not be considered as the consequence of some particular invention called 'technology' but as the consequences of what we do. Technology is not something external to us that affects our behaviour, it is essentially the form of our activity. Therefore, technology conceived as something, an external force that changes our world does not exist; it is a myth. This change of focus suggests that when we evaluate the consequences of our technical activity it is fundamental to focus on the political consequences of technical innovations rather than on their ethical dimension as if that was something that existed in itself independently of what we do.

I Introduction

Humans are technological animals, not only do they shape and transform their environment as every species does to some extent, they also add to it new realities, independent objects which only exists as a result of their activities. Of course they are not the only ones, many animals build nests, dig burrows or use more or less elaborate tools, for example to crack nuts open or to hunt. Others, like ants or termites, practice agriculture and herding, domesticating members of different species, building towering structures in which they live to house their gardens and herds. Nonetheless, we have introduced into the world an unprecedented quantity of new realities which but for our activities would not exist. In the process, we transformed the world profoundly, intervening even among its most basic components, sub-atomic particles, while we also gained the ability to act beyond the limits of our planet. Humans engage in niche construction -organism driven modification of the environment- far beyond what any other species we know has done.

Simultaneously, humans are highly social animals. *Eusociality* to the side,[2] definitions of social species are controversial, often uninformative or tautological. One suggestion is that a species is social to the extent that its members' fitness depends on relations among co-specifics rather than on independent individual interactions with the environment. The degree to which a species is social understood in this way is something that can be measured along two dimensions: importance and extension. The first correspond to how important relations with co-specifics are to the fitness of an individual compared to unmediated interactions with the environment; the second concerns the number of co-specific on which this dependence rests and the relation (parent, sibling, co-worker, etc.) they entertain with the individual.[3] According to these criteria, humans are certainly the most highly social animals on this planet. Our lives, our success and failures biological or otherwise depend primarily on our relations with others. Whether it is reproduction, business success, life expectancy, resistance to disease, cognitive abilities or any dimensions of our existence, including those we like to think of as 'natural', our performance or 'endowments' are socially mediate by direct or indirect relations to other humans.

It is likely that these two characteristics, high sociality and technical activity both complex and far reaching, are closely related. Especially as the growing complexity, number and importance of technical artefacts and networks, has gone hand in hand, not only with the augmentation in the number of humans, but also in the size of human agglomerations and in the complexity of the social relations found there. Of course, correlations are not causes and that the two things are related does not explain what their relation is. However, the importance and centrality of technology in human life, the extent to which it is inseparable from human sociality argue that whatever technology may be, it is not a 'third party'. That is to say, it is not an external force in a game played between humans and nature, but part of the very way we are who we are. To put it otherwise, it seems clear that the artificial is natural to us.

II Reflections on Technology

Hegel in 1807 formulated a view of our relation to nature and to each other that was to have a lasting influence on reflection on technology whether critical or eulogizing. In the *Phenomenology of Mind*, he argues that work, the human activity that transforms nature, constitutes both the means by which the mind re-appropriates the world which it originally posits as exterior and different from itself, and the means by which the slave regains the freedom that he lost when he submitted to the Master for fear of being killed. Hegel installed work at the heart of two fundamental human projects, liberation from natural constraints, from disease, poverty and ignorance on the one hand, and political freedom on the other. Through his conception of work these two projects became intertwined. For the next one hundred and fifty years at least, work became the fundamental topic in reflections on technology. Beyond the central place that Hegel had given it, this was due first to the fact that work is inseparable from techniques and technology and second that during the 19th century transformation of the workplace was where the impacts of technological change were most evident and far reaching.

Much of those reflections on technology (and work), beginning with Marx's, were highly critical of the consequences of technical changes. Rather than liberating us, technology was seen by many, as a source of alienation from nature and from each other. Yet, whether it was critical or believed in the promises of technology, this literature retained from Hegel the close relationship between technology and alienation, both political and in relation to nature. Very few authors – Gilbert Simondon is one of the few names that comes to mind – pursued a philosophy of technology focused on conceptual and philosophical questions, rather than on issues of alienation either political or personal.[4] Technology was analysed with a view towards its social, political and ethical consequences, but the question of what it is in itself was rarely addressed and its anthropological dimension continued to be understood in the context of work as the means through which we transform nature.

That began to change with the rise of the ecological movement in the early 1970s. The centre of attention started to shift away from man, his destiny either personal or collective, to nature as an object of moral concern. Nature as something that we need to take care of and towards which we have obligations. Either because the damage we inflict upon it will ultimately rebound upon us, or because it has a value in itself that deserves to be preserved. Nonetheless, the question of alienation remained present and important. However, from that point on it was our relation to nature, rather than political liberation, that provided the norm of the good life and of political responsibility. The workplace lost its centrality as the prime example of the negative effects of modern technology and workers their fundamental role in shaping our political future. To a large extent, this transformation of philosophical and social reflections on technology was 'event-driven', due to evolution in technologies which became more powerful, and as their ecological consequences became more evident. Furthermore, transformation of the workplace, automation and the development of service industries, rather than to universalize the working class, reduced its social and political importance.

Progressively technology came to appear more and more as something that exists and acts by itself, independently of us, an external force and a destiny which we cannot escape, that is either feared or embraced. Reflections that exalt the power and prowess of technological innovations present them as a means to 'improve nature'[5] or to go 'beyond humanity',[6] to override the limits of nature or of human nature. Positive eugenics and genetics enhancements, it is argued, will allow us to increase our physical and cognitive abilities, while Transhumanism promises us immortality. To the opposite technology is also often seen as a purely destructive force, not only in relation to nature but also to humankind. Technological progress is expected to make us redundant; the future will not need us, as Bill Joy famously claimed.[7] Or worst, AI will one day take over the world and destroy humanity.[8]

III Technology?

Limited as they were because of their quasi-exclusive focus on work and their disregard for ecological issues, earlier reflections on technology had one advantage: subsumed under the concept of work, technology is construed as a human activity, one among others, rather than as something. It is clear that there exist many technical objects, from humble water faucets to terrifying intercontinental ballistic missiles, but it is not clear that there is such a *thing* as technology. The word, in its proper sense, designates a body of knowledge, knowing how and knowing that, which relates to particular activities, for example, boat building or plumbing and it further refers, as part of technology, to the instruments and machines used in carrying out these activities. We also use the term to refer loosely to an extremely wide variety of human made objects, some of which, like an algorithm, are no thing at all. What these objects have in common is extremely abstract and difficult to pin point. Perhaps that they are the products of human activities and used in carrying out either the activity that produced them or some other activity. However, these activities are extremely diverse ranging from measuring air pressure to crowd control, from extracting ore to mail distribution, from designing video games to curing disease.

Moreover, the objects, skills and knowledge involved in carpentry seem too different from what is necessary say, to construct a plane for them to constitute together a homogeneous class. That is, a set of realities that share common characteristics distinguishing them from other sets of objects, skills and knowledge, and this is clearly the case for just about any other example one can think of. Placing the word 'modern' before 'technology' does not improve the situation. The variety of activities involved makes it impossible to think that technology constitute what philosophers call a 'natural kind', a set of phenomena characterized by uniquely shared traits. Technologies are a strange hybrids, disparate collections of human activities, of objects, the tools, buildings, vehicles related to them and of the knowledge necessary to carry out those activities. To imagine that the collection of all such collections forms a unified or coherent whole is to dream. It follows that there is no one thing that is technology, which exists in itself, that has its own particular characteristics, and which may either save or destroy us. That idol does not exists. Technologies are the means and products of human activities immensely varied throughout history and in the present.

Many recent reflections on new technologies are formulated in terms of ethics: for example, the ethics of nanotechnology,[9] of protocells,[10] of genetic manipulation[11] or of social robotics.[12] Important as some of the questions they raise may be, these approaches tend to hide the political dimension of technological transformations. Or when they are aware of it, that political dimension is reduced to the effects of innovations on common welfare, employment or the environment. Regulations are then conceived as a way of mitigating those consequences, and ethics as a code that determines the proper use of the technologies. What is overlooked in such approaches is the fact that technological changes are not simply something that happens, the sudden appearance of new objects and tools in our environment, but result from what people do, from the choices they make and from the objectives that are pursued by various social actors. What needs to be addressed are not only consequences of new technologies on nature or employment, but also the choices that lead to them and most importantly how they transform power relationships. To put it otherwise, it is not things, it is not objects that need to be regulated, but actions. Changes in relations between persons, changes with which we need to agree or to disagree should be at the heart of our reflection on technological innovations, especially as these changes in interactions often are modifications of existing power relationships whose unbalance they entrench, rather than they represent something radically new. For example, the ethical dilemma created by the technical possibility of surrogate motherhood may seem completely unheard of, but there is little new in the power relations involved between those who can, through money or power, impose their will upon others who may suffer harm and those submit either out of necessity or desire for income. To reduce this issue to a purely ethical question without taking into account its political aspect is to misunderstand and to misrepresent technological activities which inseparably are forms of interactions among social groups and individuals.

Ethical reflections tend to view issues concerning new technologies as individual questions: do I want to do this (use plastic bags, buy a smartphone, join Facebook, create protocells) or not? Questions which are addressed either to consumers or to scientists and to understand legislation, or regulation, as a means of protecting the individual while granting him or her the widest possibility of choice. A political approach to the opposite sees the issues involved as inherently relational. What is as stake in technological changes is never the single individual only, but a relational structure where agents do not act independently of others and where the aggregation of their actions may turn out to defeat the goals aimed at by the individual. Technological activities in all their forms inevitably are collective enterprises, even in very simple societies they rest on knowledge that others possess and tools that others have made.

IV Technologies and Affordances

Some years ago the American psychologist J.J. Gibson introduced the idea of affordances. Affordances are not things, they are not objects as such but what individual objects or different arrangements of objects offer to our activities, what they 'afford' an organism in terms of its actions and goals. More precisely Gibson argues that what we and other animals first perceive are not objects, but affordances, not a seat but a place to sit, not a door but an opening or an escape route, not an overhanging rock but protection from the rain, and so on. Affordances are more abstract and more general than objects, a hiding place is not any thing in particular, but instantiates an abstract relation between me and the world. Clearly affordances correspond to and highlight certain objective aspects of the world, the ground will only hold me if it is solid enough. However, they cannot be identified with those objective characteristics, because affordances only arise, so to speak, at the meeting point, at the interface of an organism, its abilities and objectives and its environment. In that sense affordances are more like events than objects, as I run pass a bifurcation my escape route disappears. It is not there anymore. Of course there is a sense in which we can say that it still exists potentially, there still is an opening there through which I can flee in thought and imagination, but in the actuality of my action, I cannot anymore. What exists potentially in that way is infinite in number, more to the point indefinite. That is, it remains unknown and under-determined until it is revealed and created as an affordance by an organism's intervention. Thus, an affordance only exists inasmuch as some organism makes it real by taking advantage of this or that characteristic of the environment.[13] To live in a world of affordances is to live in a meaningful world, but because affordances are like events predicated on an individual's action, rather than objects, this meaning is essentially subjective.[14]

It is interesting that many technical objects can be viewed as crystallized affordances, as materializing into an independent object the abstract relation to the world that defines an affordance. This is particularly evident in simple objects, a chair, a bed, a wall, a house. They are made because of what they afford protection, rest, comfort, and they give a material objective form to the affordance which they are. They stabilize the affordance, transforming the event into an object. Other objects, like a knife, a spear, a boat, and activities, horse back ridding or making fire, create or provide new affordances, making regularly possible what could not be done or was only occasionally available, like crossing a river. All these simple objects and not so simple practices reduce the contingency of affordances predicated on individual chance encounters with this or that aspect of the world and they introduce new affordances, new opportunities and dangers which did not exist previously. This of course is not only the case of simple objects, but also of smartphones, of computers, of airplane, or antibiotics. Technologies then may be understood as the various activities through which humans domesticate and materialize affordances, as well as the objects which result from these activities and some of the new affordances to which they give rise.

The materialization of affordances through human technical activities makes them objective in the proper sense, transforming them into particular objects. In the process technologies and technological practices give rise to a shared world of objects, to an objective reality which progressively takes, beyond each individual's collection of subjectively experienced affordances, a form that is not merely episodic. That is to say, the world that we share and is real for us is not only primarily made of objects we created and of the common practices that make them possible, rather than given as nature, but it is made available to us as real by these objects, sedimented affordances. It is true that to think that the world is real is to view it as existing independently of us, as a universe that is indifferent to our whims and desires, which exists in itself and imposes itself to us as the inescapable basis upon which can be done whatever can be done. Yet, paradoxically technical objects that we have created provide the experience of such a world much more clearly than our encounters with 'natural affordances' that are always to some extent contingent on our momentary needs or desire. A ladder reveals the objectivity of its purpose in a way that the tree, which I may also climb, does not. In that latter case, the objectivity of the world attached as it is to the occasion of the affordance tends to remain episodic compared to the materialized objectivity of the technical object. In the case of the ladder its objectivity is its very meaning and existence. The ladder exists not only as offered for recursive use by a plurality of users, but that is also the reason why it was made and exists.

The impact of technology then is simply who we are and the world as we know and have made it. Global warming is probably the clearest illustration that the impact of technology is not a particular problem caused by an object called (modern) technology, but the result of what we do.

Notes

1. F. John Odling-Smee, *Niche Construction: The Neglected Process in Evolution* (Princeton, NJ: Princeton University Press, 2003).
2. Eusociality is usually defined by the three following characteristics: cooperative brood care (including care of offspring from other individuals), overlapping generations within a colony of adults, and a division of labor into reproductive and non-reproductive groups. It is usually found in insects especially ants and termites but also exists in rare cases among crustaceans and mammals.
3. For more on this definition of social species, see Paul Dumouchel, 'Acting Together in Dis-Harmony. Cooperating to Conflict and Cooperation in Conflict,' *Studi di Sociologia* 55, no. 4 (2017): 303–13; Idem, 'A Covenant Among Beasts: Human and Chimpanzee Violence in Evolutionary Perspective,' in *Can We Survive Our Origins?: Readings in René Girard's Theory of Violence and the Sacred*, ed. Pierpaolo Antonello and Paul Gifford, *Studies in Violence, Mimesis, and Culture* (East Lansing: Michigan State University Press, 2015), 3–24.
4. Gilbert Simondon, *Du mode d'existence des objets techniques* (Aubier: Editions Montaigne, 1958).
5. Michael J. Reiss and Roger Straughan, *Improving Nature? The Science and Ethics of Genetic Engineering* (Cambridge [England]; New York, NY: Cambridge University Press, 1996).
5. Allen E. Buchanan, *Beyond Humanity? The Ethics of Biomedical Enhancement* (Oxford; New York: Oxford University Press, 2011).
6. Bill Joy, 'Why the Future Doesn't Need Us,' *Wired*, 2000, https://www.wired.com/2000/04/joy-2/, reprinted in Deborah G. Johnson and Jameson M. Wetmore, Technology and Society: Building Our Sociotechnical Future (Cambridge, MA: The MIT Press, 2009), pp. 69-91.
7. Nick Bostrom, *Superintelligence: Paths, Dangers, Strategies*, First edition. (Oxford, England: Oxford University Press, 2014).
8. Dónal O'Mathúna, *Nanoethics: Big Ethical Issues with Small Technology*, Think Now (London ; New York: Continuum, 2009).
9. Mark Bedau and Emily C. Parke, *The Ethics of Protocells: Moral and Social Implications of Creating Life in the Laboratory, Basic Bioethics* (Cambridge, Mass.: MIT Press, 2009).
10. Allen E. Buchanan, A. Brock, D. W. Daniels, N. & D. Wilker (eds) *From Chance to Choice Genetics and Justice*. Cambridge University Press, 2000.
12. Wendell Wallach and Colin Allen, *Moral Machines: Teaching Robots Right from Wrong* (Oxford ; New York: Oxford University Press, 2009).

13. James J. Gibson, *The Ecological Approach to Visual Perception* (Hillsdale, N.J.: Lawrence Erlbaum Associates, 1986).

14. Affordances as such are not subjective, but real: an opening is or is not sufficiently large for an animal. What is subjective, or what does not need to be more than subjective, is the animals world, what Uexküll called its Umwelt.

The Ideals of Humanity in the Light of Synthetic Biology and Artificial Intelligence

BENEDIKT PAUL GÖCKE

We shall very soon be in a position, not only to alter the biological nature of human beings and their environment genetically and cybernetically, but in addition, through the application of artificial intelligence, radically to transform individual and social life. If we are to be able to direct these technological developments and make intelligent use of their potential, comprehensive philosophical and theological theories must be produced that encompass the whole field of the position and development of human beings in the universe and give us ideals by which we can determine the negative and positive use of these technologies as a means to achieving these ideals.

I The potential of artificial intelligence and synthetic biology

In recent decades developments in theoretical and practical sciences have led to discoveries that have enabled us, for the first time in the history of humanity, not only to shape individual and social life by the application of artificial intelligence in a way previously unheard of, but in addition even to alter the human body and its environment genetically and cybernetically through the new discoveries in the natural sciences, especially in synthetic biology.[1]

1.1 The potential of artificial intelligence

In order to understand why artificial intelligence has the potential to reshape the lives of individuals and society in a radical way, we must first outline the concept of artificial intelligence. An artificial intelligence is a virtual machine whose existence is the product of human skill. Like any other machine, artificial intelligences are developed to perform a specific task: 'Artificial intelligence is a part of computer science and our aim is to build useful systems, as in any domain of engineering.'[2] The difference from classical machines such as a locomotive is that they accomplish the tasks for which they have been constructed in a way that, in the case of a human being, would require consciousness and intelligence. If intelligence is understood as the ability to attain complex goals autonomously, artificial intelligence means a virtual machine produced by human beings that can attain complex goals autonomously.[3]

In order to produce such a virtual machine, the first step is to set the goal the artificial intelligence is to attain. This is done in so-called computational theory, which provides an abstract definition of the task to be performed by the artificial intelligence, which may be, for example, to recognise individual faces or to steer a robot autonomously through an obstacle course. After the goal has been set, a way must be devised for input relevant to the task to be identified and translated into machine-readable language. Depending on the task, the output of the artificial intelligence must be translated back into a language that allows it to fulfil its task. This takes place in *representational theory*. By the use of algorithms, the virtual machine, like any computer programme, generates a specific output on the basis of a determined input. Algorithms must therefore be defined that the artificial intelligence can use to perform its task.[4] These algorithms are thus the core of any artificial intelligence. Finally, a decision must be taken about how and on what physical hardware the virtual machine is to be run.[5]

Various approaches can be identified in research that allow computer programmes to be developed using the model mentioned and brought to the point where they can autonomously attain complex goals. Alongside so-called expert systems, which, by referring back to their data banks and using logical inference rules, generate a precisely defined output for a specific input, and alongside evolutionary processes for identifying algorithms suitable for a task, there are approaches that construct virtual machines based on the way the human brain operates and which can therefore be described as artificial neural networks.

The differences between the individual approaches have to do essentially with the processes by which the input necessary for the task to be performed by the artificial intelligence is processed within the system, and so also the process by which the output is generated. Artificial neural networks frequently operate with probabilities and thus produce their results in a different way from rule-based expert systems, from which it follows that artificial neural networks are generally suited to different tasks from expert systems.[6]

The feature the various approaches to AI research have in common is that they in principle possess the ability necessary to attain complex goals: *the ability to learn from past behaviour*. From this perspective the long-term goal of AI research is to develop artificial intelligence that not only learns to operate in the world with complete autonomy, but is also perceived by human beings as an independently thinking being. Rodney A. Brooks describes this aim inn very similar terms: 'to build completely autonomous mobile agents that co-exist in the world with humans and are seen by those humans as intelligent beings in their own right'.[7]

The idea of machines capable of learning was discussed by Alan Turing as long ago as the 1950s and has subsequently, despite some setbacks, has been continuously discussed and taken further.8 However, substantive advances in the learning capacity of virtual machines, discussed under the term *machine learning*, could not be achieved before the last few decades. This is the result of the improved learning capacity of the processors now available and the availability of large quantities of data necessary for some forms machine learning – *big data* – made possible by the increasing networking of humanity through the increasing use of 'smarter' technologies.

Developmental psychology suggests at least three ways in which an artificial intelligence can continuously learn, by means of parameters supplied, to improve its performance until it reaches its maximum learning capacity; these are supervised learning, unsupervised leaning and reinforcement learning. In supervised learning the artificial intelligence is given positive examples for the output to be sought and continuous feedback about whether the artificial intelligence has achieved its task. When the task is, for example, to recognise bicycles, it is first shown images of bicycles with the information that these images show bicycles, before the artificial intelligence begins to check new images to see if they represent bicycles. Continuous human feedback then constantly improves the recognition process.

In unsupervised learning no target output is prescribed and the task of the artificial intelligence is based on optimistic meta-induction and only specified to the extent that different features of the input that in the past have appeared together will also appear together in the future. In other words, the primary aim of unsupervised machine learning consists in enabling the artificial intelligence to recognise correlations in the body of data supplied to it and suggest a probability that a specific feature in this body of data correlates with another specific feature. In this way an artificial intelligence – provided it has access to the necessary data – for example, on the basis of a woman's shopping behaviour can suggest the probability that the woman may be pregnant, if in the past pregnant women have shown the same shopping behaviour.

Reinforcement learning, in contrast, first gives the artificial intelligence the instruction to avoid negative feedback and look for positive feedback, and then assesses the performance of the system through positive and negative feedback as a way of training the virtual machine to perform its task as well as possible. Through reinforcement learning artificial intelligence can, for example, be given the ability to practise particular sequences of movements that are necessary or sufficient to fulfil its task.

It is the adaptive capacity of artificial intelligence that distinguishes it from all previous technologies and constitutes its enormous potential to change people's everyday lives. Depending on the task, an adaptive artificial intelligence can be run as a virtual machine on a computer and be specialised in data analysis or in cybernetics act as a steering unit and take over the physical movements of a machine that is connected to its surroundings through sensors. The theoretical area of application of artificial intelligence with learning ability thus touches on *every* area of ordinary individual and social life. Since adaptive artificial intelligence is in a position, through large bodies of data and by the use of parallel processing, to learn at a speed that far outstrips the limits and learning capacity of human beings, the potential effects of this technology on the lives of individuals and society can scarcely be underestimated.

1.2 The potential of synthetic biology

Synthetic biology is 'a new field of biology bordering on chemistry, information technology and engineering sciences whose aim is to produce new biological functions and organisms by artificial means'.[9] Research in artificial intelligence is directed primarily at the development of virtual machines that learn to solve complex problems and in this way influence the lives of individuals and society. In contrast, the discoveries of synthetic biology not only make it possible to modify the biological bodies of human beings genetically and cybernetically, but also, by the use of geological and ecological discoveries give us in principle possibilities of modifying the human environment through so-called *geo-engineering*.

The possibilities opened up by synthetic biology, like those of artificial intelligence, differ radically from previous technologies. For the first time in the history of humanity the natural evolution of human beings and their environment can be purposefully and enduringly altered, irrespective of cultural and economic influences, on a biological level. In this way the further course of the development of humanity can be removed from its previous biological and cosmological contingency and made an object of human planning.

At a *biological* level we can use pharmaceutical products and modern gene technologies to alter the physical and mental characteristics of a born or unborn individual temporarily or permanently. And through interventions in the human germline, using the 'gene editor' CRISSPR-cas9, we can, at least in principle, alter the human genome permanently so that the alterations can be passed on to the natural offspring. Recently in China it seems that the first pair of humans were born who, through the use of modern gene technology, not only are expected to be resistant to the HIV virus, but also able to pass on this resistance to their descendants. Through *cybernetics*, at least in principle we can construct prostheses that will be better than their natural counterparts. And nano-probes are being developed that can be inserted into the circulatory system to support bodily functions and so provide increased resistance to diseases and ageing processes. In the medium to long term, so we are often assured, this will enable us not only to support the natural functions of the biological body, but also to replace them with technological artefacts.

The overall goal of synthetic biology and its combination with research into artificial intelligence are seen by some researchers as logically leading to the complete superseding of the biological human body and the transformation of human beings into cyborgs. The consciousness of the cyborg, understood as a series of various algorithms, could then in theory run on a high-performance computer. Through so-called *mind uploading*, according to this view, it would be possible to live an almost unlimited life as software on a computer. On the assumption that it is really possible to generate an individual human consciousness through a computer programme, Kurzweil, for example, believes it possible that in 2099 our descendants will live a virtual or purely cybernetic existence: 'People will take the form of one or more virtual bodies on different levels of virtual reality and also in physical bodies produced by nano-technology, composed of nanobot swarms that can take new forms in fractions of a second.'[10]

II Back to the philosophy of history!

Research both in the area of artificial intelligence and in the field of synthetic biology provides instrumental reason with technologies that are qualitatively different from the technologies of the past: machines that can learn on their own to perform their tasks better than a human being could, and the possibility of using gene technology and cybernetics to treat human nature as a designer product and modify it according to one's own ideas: these were only a few years ago inconceivable outside myths, fairy tales and science fiction.

2.1 Opportunities and problems of the new technologies

Although they differ qualitatively from previous technologies and represent a new level of applied sciences, artificial intelligence and synthetic biology have one thing in common with any other technology: according to the underlying ideals they can be used for various purposes. Since the new technologies make it possible to alter the lives of individuals and society radically and permanently, they could become either the greatest danger or the greatest opportunity for the further development of humanity.

The greatest dangers associated with artificial intelligence are that we surrender morally relevant decision-making processes to an artificial intelligence that reaches far-reaching conclusions about the lives of individuals and society that human beings would not understand or would describe as morally wrong. After autonomous weapons systems, the most important here are analysis of the lives of individual human beings or individual social groups based on *big data*. In turn, the greatest danger of synthetic biology is that we may treat human beings as simply disposable and so run the risk of violating their inalienable human dignity. A person who knows how to genetically modify particular features of a human being will normally also know how to erase them.

The immediate dangers of the new technologies just mentioned are matched by the possible opportunities. Through the use of artificial intelligence we could not only structure global society so that no-one would any longer be forced to work – robots in the future can probably take over most human work[11] – but through the targeted application of the discoveries of the new technologies we could ensure that every human being enjoyed the longest possible span of healthy life and was immune to fatal diseases. Through the use of the new technologies along the lines of the so-called transhumanist agenda, we could also ensure that every human being received the opportunity to live a good life, was free from external pressures and leave every person free to follow their own goals. Stefan S. Sorgner argues: 'Transhumanists exclusively share the basic view, the contents of which have to be constantly adapted to the latest insights of philosophy, the natural sciences and technology, that the use of technologies as a rule has been in the interests of humanity and that we must therefore assume that this will continue to be the case in the future, and that the appropriate application of technologies will also increase the possibility of widening the boundaries of human existence, something that would be in our interest, since in this way the probability of leading a good life would be increased.'[12]

2.2 What are we to do? Back to the philosophy of history!

In the face of the possible dangers and opportunities, humanity is faced more urgently than ever by the question how artificial intelligence and synthetic biology *ought* to be used responsibly in the light of philosophical and theological principles to shape the future individual life of human beings and society, and of humanity. In order to answer this question, metaphysical, ethical and theological ideals must be defined and justified if they are to help us evaluate the rules by which these technologies can be used to attain these ideals. This is done in the philosophy and theology of history.[13]

In contrast to history, with its empirical method, which limits itself to reconstruct the past history of humanity from the available sources, the philosophy and theology of history is concerned with metaphysical and ethical knowledge about what the universe as a whole and humanity in particular is meant to develop into. Although theories about the philosophy of history were regarded as no longer tenable in periods of the verificationist critique of metaphysics and theology and in parts of the constructivist era of post-modern thought, a glance at the current debates will soon show that in relation to artificial intelligence and synthetic biology, the argument has returned, at least implicitly, to the area of the philosophy and theology of history. Much of the debate between critics and advocates of the use of the new technologies is at its core nothing other than a replay of the debates in the philosophy of history about the nature, position and future of humanity in a developing universe, conducted in terms of the different ideals of the two sides.[14]

In order to face the opportunities and dangers of the new technologies responsibly, it will in the long run not be sufficient to regulate their use on a political level in merely negative terms, since this may well mean that the further development of humanity cannot be sufficiently guided. A responsible use will instead only be possible over the long term if we reopen debates about the whole position and development of human beings in the universe, reformulate old philosophical and theological questions about a good and successful life and in the process specify the ideals that determine what use of the technologies is conducive to attaining these ideals of humanity and what not. If we do not do this, then we deprive ourselves of any possibility of meaningful regulation of their use.[15] The way forward is therefore also a way back to the philosophy of history.

Translated by Francis McDonagh

Notes

1. See Benedikt Paul Göcke, and Frank Meier-Hamidi (ed), *Designobjekt Mensch. Der Transhumanismus auf dem Prüfstand*, Freiburg im Breisgau, 2018; and Manuela Lenzen, *Künstliche Intelligenz. Was sie kann & was uns erwartet*, Munich, 2018, for further analyses of the problems and opportunities of the new technologies.
2. Ethem Alpaydin, *Machine Learning: the new AI*, Cambridge MA and London, 2016, p. 19.
3. See Margaret A. Boden, 'Introduction', Margaret A. Boden (ed.), *The Philosophy of Artificial Intelligence*, Oxford 2005, pp 1-21.
4. The task may also consist in discovering new algorithms for tasks and incorporating them into its own programme.
5. See Alpaydin, *Machine Learning*, pp 19-22.
6. The different approaches can also be combined.
7. Rodney A. Brooks, 'Intelligence without Representation', John Haugeland (ed), *Mind Design II: Philosophy, Psychology, Artificial Intelligence*, Cambridge MA and London, 1997, p. 401. The question whether we are in a position to develop an artificial intelligence that can not only perform individual tasks better than a human being, but also greatly outstrips general human intelligence, cannot be discussed here, but see Nick Bostrom, *Superintelligence. Paths, Dangers, Strategies* (Oxford, 2014) for an analysis of the problems and opportunities for the further development of humanity associated with the possible existence of a super-intelligence.
8. See Alan Turing, 'Computing Machinery and Intelligence', Margaret A. Boden (ed.), *The Philosophy of Artificial Intelligence*, Oxford, 2005, pp 40-66, for a classical analysis of performance and adaptive capacity of artificial intelligence.
9. Peter Gruss, 'Bio, Nano, Info, Neuro – Ein Panoptikum', Tobias Hülswitt and Roman Brinzak (ed.), *Werden wir ewig leben? Gespräche über die Zukunft von Mensch und Technologie*, Frankfurt, 2010, pp 35-56, 51.
10. Ray Kurzweil, *Homo Sapiens. Leben im 21. Jahrhundert – Was bleibt vom Menschen?*, Cologne, 2000, p. 359.
11. See Jerry Kaplan, *Artificial Intelligence. What Everyone Needs to Know*, Oxford, 2016, pp 114-115.
12. Stefan L. Sorgner, *Transhumanismus. Die gefährlichste Idee der Welt!?*, Freiburg, 2016, pp 9-10.
13. On the theology of history, see the essays in Georg Essen and Christian Frevel (ed.), *Theologie der Geschichte – Geschichte der Theologie*, Freiburg, 2018.
14. See Max Tegmark, *Life 3.0. Being Human in the Age of Artificial Intelligence*, New York NY and London, 2017; and Francis Fukuyama, *Our Posthuman Future: Consequences of the Biotechnology Revolution*, New York, 2002, for analyses of the new technologies from different positions that are implicitly based on ideas from the philosophy and theology of history.
15. On this, see H. Tristram Engelhard, Jr., 'Die menschliche Natur: Kann sie Leitfaden menschlichen Handels sein? Reflexionen über die gentechnische Veränderung des Menschen', Kurt Bayertz (ed.), *Die menschliche Natur. Welchen und wieviel Wert hat sie?* Paderborn, 2005, pp 32-51.

Artificial Intelligences, Robots, Bio-engineering and Cyborgs: New Challenges for Theology?

PAOLO BENANTI

Looking at the great transformations that this new stage of technology is producing, I ask if these 'new artefacts' are simply instruments or perhaps also 'sites' of our life that demand new anthropological and theological reflection. To do this I shall first introduce some new artefacts that seem to be key elements of these transformations and secondly I shall try to bring out some of the questions or issues the achievements of these technologies presents to philosophical and theological investigation. The conclusions seek to highlight how, in order to engage with the challenges technology confronts us with, we must first understand it not only as an instrument but also as a theological 'site'. In order to live in today's world we are called upon to reformulate the truths of the faith in a way that allows them to illuminate and give meaning to these 'new artefacts' and the challenges these present. We are called upon to think theologically about technology also to understand more deeply the mystery of God and the human vocation. In addition, technological developments on these unexplored frontiers requires more than ever today interdisciplinary debates and contributions, including those of theology, if we are to find adequate ends for the innumerable means it has at its disposal.

The evolution of the computer and the spread of information technology have had a deep influence on the whole world of technology, transforming our way of envisaging, producing and using technological artefacts. At the beginning, in the fifties of the last century, it seemed to be an instrument reserved for big organisations, public departments, scientific research and military command centres. Instead, the development of micro-processors from the 1970s, the constant development of accessible software and, in the 1990s, the rapid expansion of the internet have transformed the computer into a machine accessible to all, just like any other piece of household equipment. To understand this change we need to dwell for a moment on the main characteristic of this new form of communication – the fact that it is digital.

In information technology and electronics 'digital' refers to the fact that all data are represented by numbers or that operations are performed on data by manipulating numbers (digits). A determined set of data is represented in digital form, that is, as a sequence of numbers taken from a set of discrete values, or belonging to a single, well-defined and limited set. Currently 'digital' can be considered as a synonym of 'numeric' and is contrasted with the form of representing data known as analogical. Information, its digital expression and the artefacts that derive from this allow us to produce artefacts and bio-technologies unimaginable only a few decades ago.

Looking at the great transformations that this new stage of technology is producing, I ask if these 'new artefacts' are simply instruments or perhaps also 'sites' of our life that demand new anthropological and theological reflection. Is managing innovation only an issue for engineering that at most poses questions for professional ethics, or does the world of (bio) technologies also pose questions for theology?

For the purposes of our discussion I shall first introduce some new artefacts that seem to be key elements of these transformations and secondly I shall try to bring out some of the questions or issues the achievements of these technologies raise for philosophical and theological investigation.

I New artefacts

(a) Machina sapiens?

The technological development of information and the world understood as a series of data takes place in *artificial intelligences* (AI) and robots: we are in a position to construct machines that can take autonomous decisions and coexist with human beings. We might think of the self-driving cars that Uber, the well-known private transport service, is already using in some cities such as Pittsburgh or systems of radiation surgery like Cyberknife or the robots designed to work alongside human beings in production processes in factories. Artificial intelligences, these new technologies, are spreading everywhere. They are entering every area of our existence. They are both in production systems in the form of robots and in management systems, where they are replacing the analysts' servers. The latest generation of smartphones all come with an assistant endowed with artificial intelligence, *Cortana, Siri* or *Google Hello* – to mention only the main ones – that transform the telephone from a hub of services and applications to a true partner in the full sense that interacts cognitively with the user. Systems of artificial intelligence, bots, are under development that will be able to act as virtual partners that ask questions by voice or chat and able to provide services that were previously the exclusive competence of specific professions: lawyers, doctors and psychologists are always more efficiently replaceable by bots endowed with artificial intelligence.

Today the world of work is reaching a new frontier, the interactions of human beings and artificial intelligences. But before going further into the meaning of this transformation we must consider a cultural implication that risks diverting our understanding of the subject. In the development of artificial intelligences (AI) the reporting of the successes obtained by these machines has always followed the model of competition with human beings. So IBM presented *Deep Blue* as the artificial intelligence that in 1996 succeeded in defeating the reigning world chess champion Gary Kasparov, and in 2011 IBM created *Watson*, which defeated the champions of a famous American TV quiz show, *Jeopardy!* These media appearances could make us think that these are systems in competition with human beings and that a new rivalry has been created between *Homo sapiens* and this new *Machina sapiens* that will leave only one winner and condemn the loser to inevitable extinction. In reality theses machines were never constructed to compete with humans but to create a new symbiosis between human beings and their artefacts = (*homo* + *machina*) *sapiens*.[1] It is not artificial intelligences that threaten human beings with extinction, even if technology has been dangerous for our survival as a species: human beings have already threatened themselves with extinction by a very stupid machine in the shape of the atomic bomb. Nevertheless there are extremely delicate challenges in our society in which the most significant variable is not intelligence but the lack of time to make decisions, and here cognitive machines could be extremely useful.

At this level a whole series of ethical problems appear on how to validate the machine's cognition given the speed of the response and implementation sought. Nonetheless the greatest danger does not come from artificial intelligences in themselves but from a lack of knowledge of these technologies and allowing decisions on their use to be taken by a ruling class absolutely unprepared to manage this situation.

(b) Synthetic life

On 5 August 2013 over 200 journalists packed London's Riverside Studios, for the launch, not of a new smartphone or other piece of electronic kit, but of a sandwich, a hamburger, to be precise, though one that was no less astounding than a computer from a technological standpoint.

The hamburger in question was the *creation* of Professor Mark Post, a lecturer in biotechnology at the university of Maastricht, who had produced it using synthetic meat (or artificial meat or in *vitro* meat). The meat, prepared by chef Richard McGeown of Couch's Great House restaurant in Polperro, Cornwall, was tasted by the food writer Hanni Ruetzler, a nutrition specialist from the Future Food Studio, and food writer Josh Schonwald.[2]

We are trying to understand the *nature* of this *unnatural* product. The team of Dutch biotechnologists had produced an animal meat product that had never been part of a living animal. In fact, this deliberately provocative assertion would only be true if we ignore the fetal serum of a calf used as the biological basis. Fetal bovine serum, FBS, or FCS, fetal calf serum, is a liquid derived from the blood plasma that remains after the blood has coagulated or, in the technical terms, from the conversion of fibrogen into fibrin. Fetal bovine serum is in fact a secondary product of the beef industry obtained from the blood collected from the foetuses of pregnant cows during the slaughter process by means of a closed system of collectors that ensures that it is sterile. The Dutch team used FBS because it is regarded as a standard instrument for the maintenance of cell lines *in vitro*: FBS contains plasma proteins, growth factors, adhesion factors, mineral salts, chelators, vitamins, electrolytes and other substances that encourage the survival and multiplication of cells maintained in cultures. The tissue for the demonstration was the result of a process of culture *in vitro* carried out in May 2013 using at least 20,000 thin strips of muscle tissue produced in a laboratory and multiplied in a bioreactor. The Dutch team explained that once the process has been started, it is theoretically possible to carry on producing meat infinitely without adding new cells from a living organism. It is estimated that in ideal conditions two months of meat production in vitro could generate 50,000 tonnes of meat from ten pig muscle cells.

In the course of the presentation to the press the two tasters said that, apart from being a little less tasty than a traditional hamburger – an incidental issue that could be fixed – the artificial product was in every way and for all purposes equal to traditional hamburgers. The press response emphasised this and coined a series of terms for the new hamburger, 'test tube hamburger', 'laboratory hamburger', cultivated hamburger, proof of concept, 'cruelty-free burgers' and of course the lurid 'Frankenburger'.[3]

The cost of producing Post's hamburger was estimated at US$331,400, a sum achieved thanks to a donation of around 250,000 euros from the donor Sergey Brin, one of the founders of Google. Brin eventually recovered his money.

The creation of this food in a laboratory has given new energy to the existing debate between various academics on the nature of the technology and its significance for human existence.[4] A first question that seems to require an answer is whether the meat in question should be considered living or dead: the tissue of which the hamburger is composed grows and multiplies, but does not seem to possess the fundamental characteristics for it to be defined as living.[5] Even if the cells grow and multiply by sub-processes that are indeed part of living creatures, the strips of tissue nevertheless do not enjoy the characteristics such as irritability and assimilation that help us to distinguish the dynamics of a living being from those of an inanimate creature. The meat produced by *in vitro* maturation grows in the bioreactor but does not reproduce or possess that purposeful nature that characterises living things.

(c) Superhumans?

In recent years many neuro-psychiatric illnesses have been found to benefit from psychopharmacology; this is an area of pharmacology that studies the effect of drugs on behaviour and on the higher mental functions and has made it possible to create new drugs that are useful in various psychiatric disorders, whether by relieving the symptoms or treating the causes of the disorders themselves, especially in disorders of the neurotransmitters.[6] From the point of view of medical practice, the realisation that many disorders are found to be altering a spectrum that includes levels of functioning regarded as normal has led the way to a discussion of 'enhancement': for example, if drugs can improve cognition in people with a cognitive deficit, what could they do for people in normal health?

The possibility of intervening in supposed normality to obtain enhancement is based on the at least implicit conviction that full health is the new normal and that human beings need external resources to reach a level of happiness and realisation that we cannot achieve by ourselves. Cognitive improvement is, in its deepest anthropological root, an attempt to secure that fullness of life lost in the lives of our contemporaries.

Two main cognitive systems have been targeted by scientists in recent years as capable of pharmacological improvement, attention and memory.[7] To give a few examples, we have methylphenidate (MPH), sold as Ritalin, and amphetamines in compounds with dextroamphetamines under the name of Adderall, which can improve the attention of people with attention deficit hyperactivity disorder (ADHD), but can also improve attention in healthy people. Even though these drugs are apparently prescribed mainly for the treatment of ADHD, sales data indicate that they are not infrequently used for cognitive enhancement. Surveys on university campuses confirm this conclusion. Stimulants available only on medical prescription are currently widely used by university students as aids to study; many obtain them from friends or drug dealers.[8]

In addition, an enormous amount of research has been devoted recently to the development of drugs to stimulate the memory. The drugs in question act on various stages within the molecular cascade in the brain that supports the formation of memory, including the initial induction of long-term capacity and the successive stages of memory consolidation.

While this research is directed, officially, at finding a cure for dementia, there is no reason to think that some of the products under development could improve normal memory and in particular could have a use after middle age and in older people, when a certain degree of increased memory loss is normal.[9] On the other hand, the possibility of weakening unwanted memories is another type of memory treatment, under development, for a series of syndromes such as post-traumatic stress disorder (PTSD), which may contribute to enhancement in healthy individuals: theoretically it could be used as a psychological preventive, for example, to allow soldiers to go into battle or the emergency services to operate in stressful situations without collateral effects on their nervous system.[10]

II Unprecedented challenges[11]
(a) A new reality?

The first series of questions provoked by these new artefacts, which relate to philosophy as much as theology, concern reality, knowledge of reality and the difference between natural and artificial.

From the time we had not only learned to see reality as a set of data, but also learned to collect them, the big data, we had acquired a new instrument of enquiry. Three centuries ago with concave lenses we had created the telescope and the microscope, and learned to see the world in a different way. The microscope and telescope were the technological instruments with which the scientific revolution of the 16th and 17th centuries obtained its discoveries. We had made visible the extremely distant – *tele*scope – and the extremely small – *micro*scope. Today with data we have created a new 'instrument', the *macro*scope. With big data we are able to see in a new and surprising way the extreme complexity of social relations, identifying relations and connections where before we saw nothing.

Artificial intelligences applied to these enormous data-sets are the 'macroscope' that enables us to study mechanistically the extremely complex. It is up to us to understand what sort of knowledge we are creating. The key question is whether this knowledge is scientific and in what sense, deterministic or predictive. Whatever the answer, the knowledge revolution, like those of the telescope and the microscope, is already here. We are watching new challenges appear: the challenge of beginning to think of human beings as information animals alongside others, and inside the 'infosphere', the challenge of taking responsibility for a new society, the information society, which has grown much faster than the capacity of human beings to develop strong conceptual, ethical and cultural roots that enable us to understand it, manage it and direct it towards the common good and development.

In other words, we must urgently find answers to the questions of what information is, of its multiform nature, the roles it plays in various scientific contexts and answers to the social and ethical questions raised by its increasing importance. In our societies information appears in many forms and possesses many meanings. This is why many scholars today are finding it quite difficult to identify a clear and undisputed starting point; different authors have suggested different meanings for the word 'information' within the general field of information theory, but it is difficult to find a single concept of information that really does justice to its numerous possible applications described above.

We have to recognise that from a conceptual point of view the analysis of the concept of information is still in that deplorable state in which disagreement affects the very way in which the problems are provisionally formulated and contextualised in the different theoretical frameworks.

The novelty the concept of information represents in the understanding human beings have of themselves and the world is described in the following terms by Floridi:

> There is no term for this radical form of re-engineering, so we may use re-ontologising as a neologism to refer to a very radical form of re-engineering, one that not only designs, constructs, or structures a system (e.g. a company, a machine, or some artefact) anew, but that fundamentally transforms its intrinsic nature, that is, its ontology. In this sense, ITCs are not merely re-engineering but actually re-ontologising our world.[12]

Such a passage means that objects and processes are losing their very physical connotation in the sense that they are coming to be considered as independent of their own supports – we might think of a music file in MP3 format, which has become our way of understanding music as such.[13] Objects are typified, in the sense that the instance of an object – my copy of a music file, to stay with this example – is the same in type as the music file held by a third person of which my copy is an instance. In the end the criterion of existence, that is, the criterion that seeks to define what it means for something to exist, is no longer the immutable essence of its own reality, as we were led to believe by Greek thought, which held that only what does not change has full existence, or being potentially an object of perception, according to one school of modern philosophy, which has insisted on the idea that for something to count as existing is must be empirically perceptible by the senses, but being potentially subject to interaction, even if the interaction is intangible: being is being an object of interaction, even if the interaction is only indirect.

The development of biotechnologies, which are beginning to understand life itself as an information process expressed by DNA, means a crisis in the very meaning of a traditional distinction by which we understood reality, that between the real and the artificial. The amazing achievements of synthetic biology seem to result in an uncertainty, even the impossibility, of defining any boundary. The boundaries between the natural and the artificial are disappearing into thin air, leaving the two indistinguishable. The arrival of the cyborg, the amalgam of human being and machine, the birth of synthetic biology and the development of test tube meat show how everything is becoming open to manipulation and domination: the artefacts that we produce are not merely artificial, but nor are they natural.

Think of a synthetic diamond, indistinguishable from a true diamond except for two details; by law it has a serial number in its interior, engraved by laser and not visible to the naked eye, and it lacks any imperfections. We are confronted with a question that cannot be avoided by philosophy, the human sciences and by theology: are we heading for a reality in which the distinction between the natural and the artificial is destined to disappear? If this is true, what will be the consequences of this new understanding of reality? And what prospects lie ahead?

(b) A new humanity?

The far-reaching changes brought about by the sudden appearance of information and biotechnological artefacts raise new questions about human beings and their identity: anthropology becomes a key area in which philosophy and theology have to face new outlooks and unprecedented challenges. The new frontiers revealed by medicine and its translation into biotechnology have appeared in a cultural climate particularly fertile and welcoming for this type of manipulations. By the end of the last century, in fact, an intellectual trend had been produced that was favourable to technological modifications of human life, *post-human* and *trans-human* philosophy.

The vision of human beings as *malleable* creatures is one of the main forces behind *post-human* and *trans-human* thinking. A whole series of aspects that help to make our lives something never completely defined and so open to innumerable transformations, which make our existence, in Zygmunt Bauman's phrase, a 'liquid life',[14] are very relevant to this way of understanding human beings with particular emphasis on the fact that the human body itself is characterised by a certain malleability.[15] The biological make up of our bodies not only evolves, but can also be modified. The advocates of human enhancement stress the way many practices already generally accepted and widespread in medicine are in fact enhancements: vaccines, they say, are the irrefutable example of the fact that enhancements have always been accepted and used in our society.[16]

Because human beings and the universe are characterised, according to the *post-humanists* and *trans-humanists*, by complete malleability, the ability to control becomes the indispensable prerogative for ensuring our species' ability to survive.

The value of the human is no longer the person but the data that reside in their biological body: every human being is regarded as a data set contained in a medium that is their body. The human being's value is expressed in terms of data and its essence is expressed in terms of data, its essence becomes something as computable and manageable as an information flow. Life itself becomes the ability to preserve and process information. The malleability of human beings is thus transformed into a substantial devaluation of the body and its bodiliness, which come to be regarded as an *accidens* of existence.

What is it that makes us unique as human beings? How do we explain today's world the dignity of human life? What is the value of bodiliness? All these are questions that demand new approaches. The truths of the faith must be able to shed light on the new challenges that the new artefacts present to our understanding of the world and of ourselves.

If this reduction of the human person to data is in fact a new form of dualism, between the data and the medium that transmits it, it can be faced only by an anthropologically correct understanding of the body and human bodiliness. Ethnical discernment about cognitive enhancement can only succeed through an anthropological confrontation that enables the two sides to recognise the value of the body and bodililessness for human existence. In this confrontation, therefore, cognitive enhancement technology cannot be presented as an *anthropologically neutral* element, that is, a mere add-on to the anthropological discussions, but has to be rescued in all its power and complexity since we know that technical skill and technology is not what allows us to penetrate the mystery of the human being, but only ask vague questions about the 'phenomenon' that is the human being in the world. Theological thinking, in contrast, can open human beings up to their wider dimension and see in Jesus of Nazareth the exemplary human being, the only one who can reveal humans to humans. He is in fact the last human being, the *eschaton Adám*, in that he takes human beings into their future.[17]

Human life is endowed with a *telos*, a goal; it is pointed towards a dimension that is beyond time and space: theology reminds human beings of their eschataological call. In the debate with *post-human* and *trans-human* ideas we need to be able to decode the points at which cognitive enhancement is transformed into a sort of *illegitimate eschatology*: we have to confront and refute the immanentist drift that strips human beings of their future, that is, of their eschataological eternal life, and leaves them in a dream, a sort of illusion of an immortality produced by technology.

III Final thoughts

In the light of what we have seen from this survey, it seems clear that the phenomenon of technology is first and foremost a philosophical and theological 'site' that questions our understanding of the world and human nature. In order to understand technology we have to start from the awareness of a unique feature displayed by our species: as members of the species *Homo sapiens* we are symbolic creatures, endowed with responsive and flexible language. This characteristic has allowed us to cooperate with other individuals on a large scale. This is a demonstrable peculiar and irreducible characteristic that sets humans apart from every other species in existence. Thanks to this *cognitive condition*, human beings can review and modify their own behaviour rapidly, in response to changing conditions. What we can now prove to have happened is that a special form of evolution has characterised the human species as opposed to any other: cultural evolution supersedes slow and unpredictable genetic evolution. As a result of this characteristic our species began a journey that shows, from the archaeological record, an increasingly marked difference from all other species.

In talking about a 'cognitive condition' I do not wish to imply that the biological constitution of human beings has lost its influence, but we have to recognise that it is only in the case of human beings that we can talk of something that significantly transcends mere biological and genetic fact. We can summarise the relationship between biology and culture by saying that for human beings biology establishes basic parameters of behaviour and in terms of ability the whole of human history takes place within the limits of this biological space. Nevertheless it is undeniable that this setting is extraordinarily wide, allowing us to change our behaviour and social abilities in order to adapt to all the climates on earth and construct vast social groups unimaginable for any other species.

Within this unique cognitive condition that enables our species to interact with reality in a unique way – through language and culture – human beings give their actions particular purposes. Human beings relate to the world through the works of their hands – artefacts.

Technological artefacts, the basic element of technology, are coexistent with human beings and are the trace of their unique existential condition: the human condition, we can say, is a *techno-human condition*.

In the light of these facts, then, we can perhaps see the need, if we are to live up to the challenges that technology confronts us with, to look at technology, not only as an instrument, but also as a theological 'site'. To live in the present we are called on to *reaffirm* the truths of the faith in a way that lets them shed light on and give meaning to the 'new artefacts' and the challenges they pose to us. We are called on to think about technology in theological terms if we are to have any hope of reaching a deeper understanding of the mystery of God and the vocation of men and women. Beyond technological development, on these unknown frontiers, we need today as never before interdisciplinary debates and contributions, including theology, if we are to find ends adequate to the innumerable means that technology has at its disposal.

Translated by Francis McDonagh

Notes

1. Cf. John E. Kelly III, Steve Hamm, *Smart Machines : IBM's Watson and the Era of Cognitive Computing*, New York NY, 2014, pp 1-22
2. Cf. W. Galusky, 'Technology as Responsibility: Failure, Food Animals, and Lab-grown Meat', *Journal of Agricultural & Environmental Ethics* 27, 6 (2014), 931–948.
3. Cf. L. PETETIN, 'Frankenburgers, Risks and Approval', *European Journal of Risk Regulation* 5, 2(2014), 168–186.
4. Cf. P. BENANTI, *La condizione tecno-umana. Domande di senso nell'era della tecnologia*, Bologna, 2016.
5. Cf. P. BENANTI, *Ti esti? Prima lezione di bioetica*, Assisi, 2016.
6. In medicine the term psychoactive drugs covers all those drugs that act on the central nervous system. They can be classified on the basis of the type of molecules (pharmacological classes) or by their therapeutic effect. The most widely used are anxiolytics, antidepressives and neuroleptics (or antipsychotics), all of which vary in their composition. To these can be added lithium salts and anti-epileptic drugs used as mood stabilisers, and hypnotics.
7. For a detailed examination of the development of the idea of 'enhancement', see P. Benanti, *The Cyborg. Corpo e corporeità nell'epoca del postumano*, Assisi, 2012, pp 81-142, and *Neuropharmacology* 64 (2013), 1-596 (an issue of this prestigious review devoted entirely to cognitive improvement).
8. Cf. C.I. Ragan, I. Bard, I. Singh, 'What Should We Do about Student Use of Cognitive Enhancers? An Analysis of Current Evidence', *Neuropharmacology* 64 (2013), 588-595.
9. Today for the first time drugs are being developed specifically for enhancement. Examples are MEM 1003 and MEM 1414, pharmaceutical preparations currently in the final stage of testing by the US Food and Drug Administration (FDA), the government body responsible for regulating food and pharmaceutical products. These substances are being synthesised and studied to produce enhancement of human memory, and on the basis of the first tests seem to be showing surprising results; if the FDA gives a favourable opinion they could be on sale in a very short time. However, MEM 1003 and MEM 1414 are not only proving effective in improving human memory, making it almost infallible, but also succeeding in suppressing one of the worst symptoms of Alzheimer's disease, the memory loss caused by this incapacitating degenerative form of dementia (cf. O. Lev, F.G. Miller, E.J. Emanuel, 'The Ethics of Research on Enhancement Interventions', *Kennedy Institute of Ethics Journal* 20 (2010), 101-114).
10. Cf. R.M. De Bitencourt, F.A. Pamplona, R.N. Takahashi, 'A Current Overview of

Cannabinoids and Glucocorticoids in Facilitating Extinction of Aversive Memories: Potential Extinction Enhancers', *Neuropharmacology* 64 (2013), 389-395.

11. The observations in this section follow my guidelines for theological research, which have been further developed in recent years. The were among the topics of the following publications: P. Benanti, *Realtà sintetica. Dall'aspirina alla vita: come ricreare il mondo?*, Roma, 2018; *Le macchine sapienti*, Bologna, 2018; *L'hamburger di Frankenstein. La rivoluzione della carne sintetica*, Bologna, 2017; *Ti esti? Prima lezione di bioetica*, Assisi, 2016; *La condizione tecno-umana. Domande di senso nell'era della tecnologia*, Bologna, 2016; *The Cyborg: corpo e corporeità nell'epoca del postumano*, Assisi, 2012.

12. Luciano Floridi, *Information. A Very Short Introduction*, Oxford, 2010, p. 11.

13. The acronym MP3 indicates a lossy type algorithm for audio compression, developed by the MPEG group, that is able to reduce the size at the cost of some loss of the details of the sound, which drastically reduces the quantity of data required to register a sound while remaining an acceptably faithful reproduction of the original non-compressed file. Nothing material is left of the music, but it is completely contained in the digital information contained and written in the file. Of its nature the MP3 file is an approximation of reality, it is a compression algorithm that has a detail threshold – indicated as a bit-rate – beyond which the sound and its variations are ignored. While technically we may be aware of this in our modes of understanding and perception, the digitalisation and nothing else is the music.

14. See his analyses in Zygmunt Bauman, *Liquid Life*, Cambridge, 2005.

15. On this question see the following specific contributions: R. Pepperell, *The Posthuman Condition Consciousness Beyond the Brain, Intellect*, Bristol-Portland (OR) 2003, IV; R.H. Roberts, ''Nature', Post/Modernity and the Migration of the Sublime', in *Ecotheology: Journal of Religion, Nature & the Environment* 9 (2004), 315-337 ; J. Huer, *The Post-Human Society*, Frederick (MD), 2004, p. 11.

16. Cf. C.C. Hook, 'Transhumanism and Posthumanism', *Encyclopedia of Bioethics*, vol. 5, New York (NY), 1995, pp 2517-2520.

17. F. Brancato, 'Creazione ed evoluzione. Il pensiero di Joseph Ratzinger', *Synaxis* 3 (2008), 17.

Natural Science and the Church – Inevitably Opposed?: The Perspective of Church History

DOMINIK BURKARD

Is there a correlation between religion or denomination and natural science and technology? Both studies on the 'Catholic educational deficit' in the middle of the 20th century and the old 'Black Legend' seem to point to it. The condemnation of the Copernican world view by the Church's magisterium in the 17th century is also central to the foundation myth of the natural sciences. On the other hand, historical research during recent decades into the Roman Inquisition suggest caution. This article looks at motives and criteria. Research findings give little basis for positing an inherent blanket hostility to science on the part of the Church.

In the 1960s the phrase 'Catholic educational deficit' attracted attention. After studying the choice of subjects made by students from a denominational perspective, Jesuit Karl Erlinghagen came to the conclusion that Catholics provided fewer students in all areas of study – except theology – than would be expected from their percentage in the population. They were heavily under-represented in technical areas (9,7) and the natural sciences (11.1). This study for the first time provided empirical evidence for what had been widely asserted, especially in the 19th-century culture wars, namely that there was a denominational 'backwardness', even an 'inferiority' among Catholics with regard to education and science, and that in fact Catholicism was incompatible with 'the modern world'

Attempts to explain these findings range from the economic and social or arguments from educational policy to causes that allegedly lie in theology itself. These include the tendency of Catholicism to be based in predominantly agricultural and rural societies, the importance attached to the 'sacred' with an associated extensive culture of feast days (which got in the way of work), an inadequate educational system, including traditional Catholic mechanisms of passing on knowledge that relied less on literacy (symbolism, ritual, worship), as opposed to the Protestant attitude of *sola scriptura*, and the long-term economic consequences of a different understanding of justification (Max Weber's 'Calvinist economic ethics'.

Erlinghagen's demonstration, in the case of German Catholicism, that a clear reluctance about technology and the natural sciences existed even in the 20th century seems completely in accord with the so-called 'Black Legend' that appeared in Spanish historiography in the 18th century and was also accepted in Portugal and Italy. According to this, in order to secure its monopoly of interpretation, the Catholic Church combated newly emerging rival systems of interpretation – therefore including the (natural) sciences with the use of repressive measures to ensure conformity, namely censorship and the inquisition. As a result of this inherent hostility to science in the Church system, so the argument goes, Catholic countries lagged behind countries influenced by Protestantism in their further cultural and social development.

But how reliable is the 'Black Legend'? Can the thesis of a dichotomy between the Church and natural science really be stood up? Using the research done into the Inquisition over the last 25 years, this article seeks to show, with examples, how the Roman Inquisition and ecclesiastical censorship (as organs of the Church's 'magisterium' or teaching authority), dealt with progress in the natural sciences.

I Physics: the 'case of Galileo Galilei' and its consequences

The best known example of the Church's 'hostility to science' is the case of the Italian polymath Galileo Galilei (1564-1642). In connection with unpublished letters that circulated in Rome after the invention of the telescope, in 1616 the Inquisition for the first time banned Copernicus' view by a decree of the Congregation for the Index. At the same time the text *De revolutionibus orbium coelestium* (1430) by the canon of Frombork

Cathedral and doctor, Nikolaus Kopernikus (1473-1543), dedicated to Pope Paul III, and the *Lettera sopra l'opinione della mobilità della Terra* ('Letter on Opinion about the Mobility of the Earth') of the Carmelite theologian and astronomer, Paolo Antonio Foscarini (1565-1616), were placed on the Index of Forbidden Books. Interestingly, the Inquisition did not condemn the Copernican thesis as heretical (that is, as obstinate denial of a revealed truth), but simply as 'false' and 'in contradiction of Holy Scripture'). *De revolutionibus orbium coelestium* was banned with the qualification *donec corrigatur*, 'until it is corrected', which allowed for the possibility of removing objectionable passages.

Something similar happened in the case the Roman Inquisition opened in 1632 against Galileo, because, in his *Dialogo sopra i due massimi sistemi del mondo* ('Dialogue on the Two Major Systems of the World') he dared to defend the heliocentric worldview. As is well known, the case ended with Galileo's recantation. In its long afterlife, the 'Galileo case' became a symbol of the Church's hostility to science and a marker for the drifting apart of religion and (natural) science. But was that a correct assessment?

The general rules of the Tridentine Index had limited themselves to banning books that dealt in astrological or magical assertions – a rule that should be understood in a completely 'Enlightenment' sense: the idea was to counter the spread of superstition.

With its ban on the Copernican system, however, the Inquisition was venturing into new territory, that of the natural sciences. The ban was quite sophisticated. Galileo claimed to be teaching incontrovertible truth. Against it there were (in the framework of contemporary discussion) serious arguments, since the geocentric system rested on everyday observation of the heavenly bodies. Moreover, Galileo's doctrine seemed to contradict biblical statements (Gen 1.16-18; Jos 10.12-14).

On several occasions the Inquisition therefore took the position that the heliocentric system could not be presented as established fact, but only as a hypothesis. Nor could further implications for the interpretation of holy scripture be drawn from it. In these decisions the validity of the mathematical and physical calculations was fully recognised, but wider conclusions, especially in theology, were rejected. That the aim was precisely to avoid polarisation is shown by the theologian and controversialist Robert Bellarmine (1542-1621), who, as president of the Congregation for the Index, in 1616 maintained the view that mathematical theses about nature could not claim absolute validity because they were based only on accidental situations, that is, on sensible phenomena that were liable to constant change. But did the *theological* censors also see the consequences of the heliocentric model, the expulsion of human beings from their position as the crown of creation, justified by the biblical creation story, and the fact that in a world explained in purely mechanistic terms God as the Aristotelian 'unmoved mover' must also be called in question?

The tension between the physical construction of the world and religious conviction in the 17th century had by no means the bitterness of a theoretical opposition that was later constructed. While in his *Discorsi e dimostrazioni matematiche* (1638), Galileo described the world as a purely mechanical system, since he took faith for granted, he never drew any atheist conclusions from that position.

Subsequently, although experiential arguments for the geocentric model were disproved only gradually as observation of the movement of the stars improved, and some were only refuted much later, the geocentric worldview became accepted very quickly. A radical paradigm shift took place: experiment alone, what is mathematically quantifiable, came increasingly to be the exclusive source of scientific knowledge and the standard of truth, while other forms of discovery, philosophical and theological reflection, increasingly incurred the odium of being unscientific and mere speculation.

In the face of this absolute status now enjoyed by physical explanations of the world, the Church clung to the metaphysical world system – including its 1616 and 1632 judgments. Benedict XIV (1675-1758) made the first attempt to free the Inquisition from the reputation of being hostile to science by undertaking a reform of the institution. Authors whose works were sent for censorship were now to be give a hearing and provided with a defender. In addition, he ordered that a ban should not be imposed on writings that defended the heliocentric system. At a time when the heliocentric view had become generally accepted as scientific knowledge, the magisterium thus showed itself completely open to agreement. Censors were no longer to be forced to take action against what had become the scientific consensus. But it was not until 1992 that Galileo was publicly rehabilitated by Pope John Paul II.

II Medicine: a 'Modernising' Roman Instruction on Witch Trials

In connection with the 'backwardness' of the Roman Inquisition, another point is usually mentioned, the phenomenon of the modern persecution of witches. The Inquisition is constantly blamed for these – and for superstitions and irrational methods of reaching the truth.

The implied connection can, however, be countered by two simple observations. First, many regional studies have shown that the widespread panic about witches was not a phenomenon specific to one denomination. Second, where the modern inquisition operated, that is, in the Latin countries, only a very few people were killed as witches. Why?

An explanation can be found from a comparison of the instruction on witches issued by the Roman Inquisition at the beginning of the 17th century and the process normal in Germany. This shows that the German procedure was based on denunciation and torture as essential elements. This is connected with the idea common in northern Europe that all witches knew each other from the 'witches' sabbath'. It followed that if a witch had been convicted, the names of other witches could be forced out of her.

While the Roman Inquisition also regarded black magic and harmful spells as in principle part of the content of witchcraft, formally scepticism prevailed with regard to the practical proof required. For this reason, the Inquisition set higher standards of proof. It demanded not only an elaborate testing of all evidence, but also provided at two points in the trial – and this is crucial – for the consultation of an experienced doctor. Whereas in northern Europe there was a belief in conspiracy and collective guilt, the Roman Inquisition had a presumption of pathological phenomena and individual cases. To do justice to this situation, it integrated medicine as a natural science into its procedures and in this way attempted, on the one hand to bring rationality to the 'witch' phenomenon, and on the other to curb its excesses with the aid of scientific knowledge.

III. Evolution: a second sin against natural science?

Copernicus had just widened humanity's gaze to the immeasurable distances of the universe, and at the moment that our University was founded, theology found itself engaged in a decisive battle, one of the greatest and most momentous of its history. It seemed, as Feuerbach blasphemously put it in the 19th century, that as the temple of nature opened with overwhelming majesty, the old God was made homeless. And yet it took another three centuries for the new world view to show the effect of all its consequences... After sight of the infinitely large came sight of the infinitely small, after the telescope the microscope... Now the hitherto firmly closed globe opened its archives and seemed to be telling a different story from bible and theology. At this theology was terrified.

It was with these words that in 1909 the Würzburg dogmatic theologian Franz Xaver Kiefl (1869-1928) began his inaugural address as rector of the university. Kiefl stressed two reasons why theology had been suspicious of all attempts 'to probe into the mystery of life with mechanistic methods'. First, the mechanical approach must take the blame for 'shallow materialistic attempts' to explain away the mysterious, the incommensurable, element in nature, and denied the transcendent character of things and all 'ideal life values that precede and underlie development'. Second, the mechanism seemed to lead 'to blind chance as the alpha and omega of the world's existence'.

It was in fact in the 19th century, above all with the discovery of evolution, that the expansion of the modern, increasingly specialised natural sciences took place, and as a result an explosion of knowledge and so to a new paradigm shift. And now once more, but this time at the height of the battle for explaining and visualising the world, the question was again posed about the compatibility of traditional biblical and religious ideas of creation and the findings of this 'modern' science.

It was especially the popularisers and 'designers' of the new knowledge that constructed a crude opposition. For example, Ernst Haeckel (1834-1919), who regarded religious belief as more of a feature of a stage of animal organisation at which the ability to think had not fully developed, and in his book *The Riddle of the Universe*, originally published in 1899, proclaimed an 'irreconcilable contradiction' between the 'superstitious belief' in a divine revelation and the 'natural religion of reason'. 'The true revelation, that is, the true source of rational knowledge, is only to be found in nature. ...Any reasonable person with a normal brain and normal senses who looks at nature without preconceptions receives this true revelation and so frees them-self from the superstition with which the revelations of religion have burdened them.'

The reaction of theology and Church to such conclusions was admittedly one of rejection. And yet people did not let themselves be dragged into rejecting *evolution as such*. This can again be seen from the practice of the Roman Inquisition. None of the writings of the leading proponents of the theory of evolution ended up on the 'Index of Forbidden Books'. Not even Haeckel – probably because of the public nature of his hostility – was given the honour of an official condemnation. Nonetheless the Church did argue against the theory of evolution itself and its prominent representatives, though only indirectly in dealing with Catholic 'evolutionists', who attempted to mediate between the discoveries of natural science and the Christian faith, or the biblical statements about creation.

A number of publications came into the sights of the defenders of the faith, including those of the French Dominican Dalmas Leroy (1828-1905). Leroy argued that the bible showed *that*, but not *how*, God had produced the various species, and accordingly the model offered by the theory of evolution for this could not be in contradiction to holy scripture. The assumption of fixed species, he argued, was no more than a popular belief based on appearances. As a witness to the 'tradition', he claimed, Augustine – with his allegorical interpretation of the creation story, his teaching on *rationes seminales*, and his beliefs about the origin of the human soul – seemed easiest to link with the theory of evolution.

In his book *Evolution and Dogma* (1896), the American Catholic priest and academic John Zahm (1851-1921) argued that life had developed in matter purely as a result of chemical and mechanical forces, the original protozoa had developed through favourable conditions and after tens of thousands of years had moved from the plant to the animal state. The same stages of constant development had accompanied the organism of the first animal, with the result that the animal had risen from the lowest forms of sensible life to a form more or less similar to that of a human being. This being, however, was not freshly created by God in its bodily form, but through the ensoulment of the body of a human-like animal, which had come into being out of inorganic matter through evolution.

A different position was argued by Henry de Dorlodot (1855-1929), a theologian and geologist at the Catholic University of Leuven, an 'absolutely natural evolution', which denied any *special* intervention by God, not only at the beginning of vegetative life, but also at the beginning of sensible and human life.

In the specific case of Dorlodot the Roman consultors and cardinals – in view of the complexity of the subject – voted to review the Church's position on the issues raised by evolution before a final decision. But this never happened. Shortly afterwards Rafael Merry del Val (1865-1930), the most senior Vatican official, gave Cardinal Mercier (1851-1926), Archbishop of Malines-Brussels, the explanation that the Holy Office did not intend to make any pronouncement on evolution *from a scientific standpoint*, nor would the Biblical Commission make a judgment on the scientific issue of the transformation of plant species or lower animal species into the human body.

This indicated where theology's real problem with evolution lay, on the field of exegesis. In reply Mercier correctly noted that 'transformism' was accepted in principle by most academics either as a theory or only as a scientific hypothesis. His suggestion, that in view of the importance of the issue a competent commission of academics, philosophers, theologians and exegetes should be set up to study the question of the origin of living creatures and the differentiation of organisms with their possible relationship to revealed doctrine, was, however, not taken up. The magisterium clearly intended to limit itself to its genuine field of competence and only to get involved where natural science went beyond its limits and strayed into the field of theology. So had lessons been learned from the Galileo case?

IV A quantitative approach: sobering findings and an attempt at an explanation.

The question whether the Roman Inquisition, as one of the most important agencies of ecclesiastical censorship, should be held responsible for making the development of natural science more difficult, can be answered in part by a quantitative analysis. For example, Ugo Baldini took the *Index librorum prohibitorum* of 1819 and noted all the publications on 'natural science' that had been condemned over a period of 250 years. He used a very broad concept of 'natural science' and took into account all works whose subject matter or methodology brought them close to our current concept of 'science'. This included specialist literature about astronomy, cosmology, mathematical physics, physical geography, anatomy, medicine, zoology, chemistry and alchemy, as well as texts on astrology with sections on astronomy, experimental physics or chemistry, but also texts on theology which gave particular attention to cosmological and scientific issues, together with encyclopedias, which played a particular role in spreading modern ideas about science.

The survey showed that between 1559 and 1819 only 124 books with 'scientific' content were placed on the index – a very small number compared to book production. This finding raises the fundamental question whether a significant correlation between published discoveries in the natural sciences and Church censorship exists at all.

There are some observations that put the result in a slightly different perspective. For example, despite its claim to represent the universal Church, the *Index librorum prohibitorum* was at least in part focused on Italy: 30% of the books on the Index were in Italian. In addition, there is a suspicion that there was a degree of unprofessionalism among the curial officials – even though members of the congregations included at times significant scientists such as the mathematician who had been influenced by Galileo, Michelangelo Ricci (1619-1682), or François Jacquier OFM (1711-1788) and Thomas Le Seur OFM (1703-1770), whose commentaries on Newton's *Principia* were among the best.

Not the least significant result of the survey is that it raises a question about the criteria for the selection of books to be placed on the Index: why and when was a text reviewed at all by the Inquisition or by the Congregation of the Index? The apparently obvious answer that the 'importance' of a text was the decisive criterion seems doubtful. The relevance of a theory is not apparent immediately but only in the course of the further development of science, making it unsuitable as a standard for use by curial officials in placing books on the Index.

Other criteria, however, can be firmly identified for the censorship of a text or theory:

(a) Theological relevance. The common assumption that scientific works were banned because of their scientific theories is in many cases false. Instead it can be shown that these texts were rejected because they – often quite incidentally (in the introduction or the dedication) contained *religiously inopportune* views. Or anatomical works might be regarded as morally objectionable; works on physics perhaps contained sections on astrology and magic. Mostly the censors had no objections to the purely scientific significance of particular theories or disciplines, but their historical or conceptual links with religious or ethical views was regarded as objectionable or dangerous. The prohibition of such texts thus had in principle little to do with their scientific contents in the modern sense.

Another factor was that to non-specialists – as most censors in the field of research in the natural sciences in fact probably were – the contradiction between a theory and traditional cosmology was not always obvious. Newton's mechanics, for example, quite apart from its implications for the structure of the solar system, turned many basic assumptions of traditional cosmology upside down, but from a theological point of view it remained an apparently 'neutral' theory. It is also astonishing that of the several hundred publications from the second half of the 17th century onwards that laid the foundations of geological chronology and palaeontology, hardly one met objections, although they had an impact on biblical chronology, and as a result the text of Genesis lost its claim to scientific and historical truth. The publications were left undisturbed because what was being examined here were phenomena, irrespective of their anthropological, philosophical or religious implications.

In other words, a distinction was evidently made between writings that were purely scientific and those that went beyond science and touched on religion itself with 'ideological' arguments. The tendency of the congregations was to intervene in organic matters rather than inorganic (geology), in anthropology rather than zoology, and within anthropology in cultural anthropology with its ideas about human behaviour and moral values, rather than in what would today be called medical anthropology. Overall the conclusion must be that the censorship was not directed at any scientific innovation, against scientific discovery in general or against an experimentally-based model of science. Objections were raised, rather, to those parts and aspects of scientific thought that represented a direct and explicit challenge to the traditional Christian world view.

(b) Alongside the criterion of theological relevance, that of publicity also played a role. In a system that allowed for a relatively large margin of discretion in the application and implementation of theological and procedural principles, expediency and the impact of a decision were fully taken into consideration. Also relevant is the observation that it was often not the works crucial to a theory that ended up on the Index, but those that helped to spread the arguments at a more popular level. So in the field of 'Cosmology, Structure of the Universe and Mechanics of the Heavens' almost only popularisations of the science were placed on the Index – with the exceptions noted above.

(c) Moreover, what was certainly taken into account was the inherently intellectual criterion of probability. Remember: Copernicus' work *De revolutionibus orbium coelestium* was not 'absolutely' banned, but *donec corrigatur*, 'until it is corrected'. In other words, Copernicus was given the opportunity to remove objectionable passages. This was possible because his technical apparatus was regarded as a series of 'mathematical' statements that were correct in themselves and by the use of which celestial phenomena could be described and predicted. However, the basic thesis of the work, of a particular arrangement of the sun and planets in space, was regarded as a scientific *hypothesis*. Logically all that required correction were the (few) sentences in the work that presented this thesis as a description of the real cosmos.

V Conclusion

Recent research on the Inquisition has been unable to substantiate the thesis of the 'Black Legend' on the link between the Inquisition and scientific backwardness. In other areas too it makes little sense to talk of a principled hostility in Catholicism towards natural science and theology.

In this connection we need only remember the natural history collections built up and preserved over centuries in monasteries and their collections of specialised literature on natural philosophy that were not transferred to the state until the 19th century. We may also remember the reform that gave us the 'Gregorian' calendar which the Pope ordered to be carried out in 1582 on purely astronomical grounds – and making practical use of the heliocentric model – in the Vatican's *Torre dei Venti*, the papal observatory, a reform that non-Catholic states only adopted after considerable delay (Prussia in 1612, Great Britain in 1752, the Soviet Union in 1918). Finally we should remember the numerous theologians who, though priests, made a name for themselves as naturalists, discoverers, doctors and technical inventors: Nils Stensen (1638-1686), Gregor Mendel OSA (1822-1894), Erich Wasmann SJ (1859-1931) or Teilhard de Chardin SJ (1881-1955) are only a few of the better-known names. In the field of astronomy well into the 20th century Jesuits were especially prominent.

The alleged inherent backwardness of Catholicism as a system also seems dubious because of the denominational characterisation; after all, all denominations played a role in the core process of modernisation. While Protestantism was quicker to recognise the autonomy of the various specialisms, on the other hand the post-Tridentine view of human beings in Catholicism seems to have been much more compatible with modern culture than Luther's idea of the complete corruption of human beings. Could this explain that in particular the Jesuits, who propagated this 'modern' view of human beings, were more interested in technical matters and had so few fears of being contaminated by contact with the natural sciences?

But there is another side. The scepticism, even contempt, that many Catholics had for the natural sciences and technology right into the 20th century, and perhaps still have today, requires an explanation. Possibly we have here to take into account the success of a pastoral approach that for a long time kept alive the idea of a hierarchy of values oriented to the next world. But if God is the ultimate ground of being and meaning, then the priority for human beings must be the realisation of their qualities in the here and now (Jesus' message of the 'kingdom of God'; Matthew 25), but not the completion of the tower of Babel (Genesis 11). The talents and abilities we have been given are not to be buried away, but put to profitable use – in this sense faith definitely has a material side. But this material side must not become an end in itself, or it will corrupt the God-given talents – and thus our human vocation.

Translated by Francis McDonagh

Dominik Burkard

Bibliography

Mariano Artigas, Thomas F. Glick, Rafael A. Martínez (ed.), *Negotiating Darwin. The Vatican confronts evolution 1877-1902*, Baltimore 2006.

Ugo Baldini, 'Die römischen Kongregationen der Inquisition und des Index und der wissenschaftliche Fortschritt im 16. bis 18. Jahrhundert: Anmerkungen zur Chronologie und zur Logik ihres Verhältnisses', Hubert Wolf (ed.), *Inquisition, Index, Zensur. Wissenskulturen der Neuzeit im Widerstreit*, Paderborn 2003, pp 229-278.

Ugo Baldini, Leen Spruit (ed.), *Catholic Church and modern science. Documents from the archives of the Roman congregations of the Holy Office and the index, Vol. 1: Sixteeenth-century documents*, Parts 1-4, Rome, 2009.

Francesco Beretta, *Galilée devant le Tribunal de l'Inquisition. Une relecture des sources*, Fribourg, 1998.

Francesco Beretta, 'Katholische Kirche und moderne Naturwissenschaft von Galilei bis Darwin. Die Voraussetzungen einer konfliktgeladenen Begegnung', Mariano Delgado (ed.), *Glaube und Vernunft – Theologie und Philosophie. Aspekte ihrer Wechselwirkung in Geschichte und Gegenwart*, Fribourg, 2003, pp 117-133.

Dominik Burkard, 'Augustinus – ein Kronzeuge für die Evolutionstheorie? (Gescheiterte) Versuche einer Versöhnung von Theologie und Naturwissenschaft', Cornelius Mayer, Christoph Müller, Guntram Förster (ed.), *Augustinus – Schöpfung und Zeit*, Würzburg, 2012, pp 109-141.

Rainer Decker, *Die Päpste und die Hexen. Aus den geheimen Akten der Inquisition*, Darmstadt, 2003.

Peter Godman with the assistance of Jens Brandt, *Weltliteratur auf dem Index. Die geheimen Gutachten des Vatikans,* Berlin and Munich, 2001, pp 43-49, 163-216.

Part Two: Technological Rationality and Post-Colonial Criticism

Persistence of Colonialism and Modern Technology: An Anthropological Reflection from an African Perspective

PETER KANYANDAGO

Modern technology has largely been associated with Western civilisation, to the detriment of other technologies. The article points out that Egyptian technology in the third millennium BCE compares by far with modern technology in its precision in the areas of architecture and astronomy, and other areas. The marginalisation of this technology, and persistence of colonialism in the same, is due largely to the anthropological negation of the African and other non-Europeans through different processes including colonisation, enslavement and evangelisation. This situation can be solved by putting in place means to rehabilitate and respect the humanity and dignity of the African.

I Introduction

Human beings have been able to design and produce increasingly complex tools, machines, equipment and gadgets, which in a sense, can be seen as the extension of the human mind and hands. Technology is intimately linked to science, religion, and worldview. We note that the most dominant, visible and prevalent type of technology which we will call 'modern', is a product of Western (European) experience, science and knowledge. This modern technology has benefited and borrowed from other types of technologies, and so there exist other types of technology, although this

63

is hardly ever acknowledged.[1] To discuss why colonialism has persisted in technology, I will first show that before modern technology there was African technology. This persistence is rooted in a generalised Western anthropological and physical negation of non-Europeans other people and their achievements, justified and reinforced by the Roman Church in the 15th century. This type of technology has been associated with, and in a sense, promoted European colonisation. So while these ethical and societal challenges are wide spread, we should not give the impression that they are 'universal', or that there are no other alternatives or are insurmountable. Our reflection includes an epistemological aspect in as far as technology is a product of science and knowledge systems. This discussion will be linked to the fact that European civilisation has been, and is, closely related to Western Christianity. I will end my contribution by suggesting that humanity will be able to solve problems coming from technology on condition that we accept to critique and very well situate modern technology, we acknowledge and use other types of technologies and that the necessary ethical and economic measures be put in place to make reparations and compensations for injustices that have been committed in the way we conceive and use technology.

II African Technology

It is now practically established that the African continent is a cradle of humanity.[2] Modern human beings have existed on the African continent from the beginning of humanity without coming from outside. This means Africans have had time to evolve appropriate means of adjusting to and using the environment. However, there are other more precise technological African achievements that need to be mentioned. The oldest known monumental sculpture in Egypt is the Great Sphinx of Gaza built between 2558 and 2532 BCE.[3] The oldest and largest pyramid in the Giza pyramid complex is the Great Pyramid of Giza, also known as the Pyramid of Khufu, said to have been constructed during the reign of king Khufu (2589-2566 BCE)

The mathematical and architectural precision of the pyramid is a feat of human prowess and ingenuity that has to be recognised, especially if we consider that the pyramid was put up at a time when the instruments of precision known to us were not available.[4] This immense technological achievement is not just a material monument: it is closely related to how ancient Egyptians viewed the life hereafter and the attention and respect they accorded the dead. Africa is also a pioneer in other scientific and technological areas, including mathematics, astronomy, metallurgy and tools, medicine, navigation, education, agriculture and textiles.[5] While many writings on the achievements of Africa in the area of science and technology focus on Egypt, and this region is better documented, Egypt must not be seen in isolation: Egypt indeed is a child of Africa.[6] Let me mention quickly that African civilisation, as a whole, is not an appendix of human history. Cheikh Anta Diop[7] and Yosef A. A. ben-Jochannan[8] have sufficiently written about this. Diop also defended and showed that ancient Egyptians were African, contrary to what many Western writers were saying.[9] If the technology alluded to has disappeared or has gone underground, there are historical and anthropological factors, external and internal, which explain this. The successive invasions BCE, followed by planned invasions, looting and colonisation of Africa by Europe in 15th century, and continued thereafter, interrupted the normal development of Africa and depleted its human and material resources, and this has continued till today, often with the collaboration of some Africans.

III Western Christian Roots of Colonisation and Negation

Western Christianity, and more specifically Catholicism, has been associated with what Europe has done to other people, the good and the bad, including colonisation, slave trade, genocides and massacres of the people who were invaded in Asia, America and Africa.[10] These processes were initially started by Catholic countries, Spain and Portugal and were later joined by England and The Netherlands, and other countries later. The acts of discovery, Christianisation and colonisation, with their attendant violent doctrines and acts were justified, and in some cases started, by official papal documents called bulls.

The Three Papal Bulls

Of these bulls three need special mention in as far as they relate to discovery, colonialism and enslavement. The first of these, *Dum diversas*, was issued by Pope Nicholas V on 18 June 1452 in favour of king Alfonso of Portugal to fight enemies of Christ. An extract from it is given here below:

65

... we grant to you full and free power, through the Apostolic authority by this edict, to invade, conquer, fight, subjugate the Saracens and pagans, and other infidels and other enemies of Christ, and wherever established their Kingdoms, Duchies, Royal Palaces, Principalities and other dominions, lands, places, estates, camps and any other possessions, mobile and immobile goods found in all these places and held in whatever name, and held and possessed by [them]... and to lead their persons in perpetual servitude, and to apply and appropriate realms, duchies, royal palaces, principalities and other dominions, possessions and goods of this kind to you and your use and your successors the Kings of Portugal.[11]

Pope Nicholas V issued another bull, *Romanus Pontifex*, on 8 January 1455. [12] This bull settled the conflict between Portugal and Castile (Spain) over who had rights to colonise, take slaves and trade in Africa and along the African coast. Pope Alexander VI issued the bull *Inter Caetera* on 3 May 1493. After Columbus had 'discovered' some islands and mainlands in the west, it appears Portugal had claims to the same. Pope Alexander VI, a Spaniard, was approached by the sovereigns of Spain, Ferdinand and Isabella, to settle the issue. Here below is an extract from the same.

...by the authority of Almighty God conferred upon us in blessed Peter and of the vicarship of Jesus Christ, which we hold on earth, do by tenor of these presents... assign to you and your heirs and successors, kings of Castile and Leon, forever, together with all their dominions, cities, camps, places, and villages, and all rights, jurisdictions, and appurtenances, all islands and mainlands found and to be found, discovered and to be discovered.[13]

Like in the previous 2 bulls, the justification of the donation is the conversion of pagans to the Catholic faith. This bull, and the 2 others mentioned above, are the most violent religious and political documents which laid foundation for the oppression, exploitation, enslavement and expropriation of all pagan non-Europeans, wherever they might be found and for all times. As far as I know, these bulls and many others related to them, have not yet been revoked by the supreme Catholic authority of the pope. If we take the 3 bulls together, especially the first two already mentioned, it is not only natural resources that were given, but also people found in those areas. The tenor of the bulls is universal in the intention and those targeted. We can see how the negation and suppression of non-Europeans are justified. The importance and implication of this are far-reaching.

Aftermath of the Bulls

What is at stake here in the first place is not theology but anthropology. Europe, especially in its being Christian sees itself having the right to enslave and colonise non-Christians. Let us note again that besides the anthropological reasons, there is always an economic reason for Europe to go out and take the resources of other people because the continent was poor. Subsequent to the coming in contact between the Europeans and non-Europeans, the 'Doctrine of Discovery'[14] was developed to justify what Europe, and eventually United States, had done to take countries that were not European and Christian. Referring to the papal bulls, being European coincided with being Christian and civilised. Here the anthropological and theological (religious) considerations go together. Not to be baptised excluded one from being a real a human being. About the same time, the category of '*res nullus*' was evolved. *Nullus* means 'nobody' or non-existent, and *res* means a 'thing'. The colonising powers assigned indigenous people to the category of *nullus*. Originally used in Roman law, *nullus* meant that at the start of war, the territory is of nobody. The enemy of the Romans was a 'nobody'.[15] Hindsale points out that the Catholic Church introduced a new category of *nullus*, namely, a claim not by conquest but by discovery: through discovery, the 'discoverer', or more precisely the invader takes the property of nobody. Hindsale notes with concern how the Church could have been at the origin of such a doctrine justifying the spoliation and enslavement of the heathen.[16] The anthropological categories are the ones which determine the theological and ethical concepts: theology does not have a language and concepts independent of the historical and anthropological milieu in which it evolves. What I say here can also be analogically applied to the scriptures. The stage is now set to appreciate better why there is persistent colonialism in the area of how technology is conceived and used in the South.

Persistence of Colonialism in Technology

In light of what has been summarised above, we are now in better position to discuss why a colonial mentality marked by negation of the value of what the non-European is or makes. At this level we are also dealing with an epistemological question: African knowledge, science and technology do exit, but are not duly acknowledged and used. The persistence of colonialism will be discussed under refusal to repatriate African precious cultural objects found in Western museums and the looting of African science, objects and technology, which is more than biopiracy.

Many of the technologies and works of art of Africa were looted during the colonial period and are now in European and American museums. On 28 November 2017, Emmanuel Macron, President of France, while in Ouagadougou, Burkina Faso, said that efforts should be made to restitute African works of art to Africa.[17] Two people, Bénédicte Savoy and Felwine Sarr, were asked to do the needful to implement this. The questions and fears raised by this work are coloured by a colonial mentality. In discussing restitution we do not hear about compensation or injustices caused to Africans: they seem to remain relegated to the category of *nulli* (plural of *nullus*). If the objects in question were unjustly taken out of Africa, returning them is not enough. There should be compensation. Secondly, the initiative to return works of art was taken by a President of a country that was involved in looting. The same country cannot justly make a proposal and offer answers. This is an indication of the colonial 'we know what is better for them' mentality. Thirdly, when the report was about to be handed over, France reacted with fear that the objects on their colonial museums would be taken away. The concern is not about doing justice but about losing plundered objects. Lastly, there are some racist insinuations that Africans do not have the technology and space to receive and look after these objects. While this might be true objectively, if there was sensitivity to people who had been deprived of their works of art, one could have imagined starting a process of creating conditions for looking after these objects instead of dismissing the idea on the grounds of missing technology, which evokes the idea of African being non-people.

Another example to illustrate the persistence of colonialism in African technology is the reopening of what was called the Royal Museum for Central Africa in Tervuren, Brussels, Belgium. This is said to be a European museum with the biggest collection of African objects. The history of this museum is marked with a violent and colonial history in regard to the Democratic Republic of Congo (DRC) from which most of the objects were taken. It has about 180,000 objects, among which are beheaded skulls of vanquished African chiefs. The museum underwent a revamp for five years at a cost of US 78 million in a bid, among other things, to shed off the colonial image, and was reopened on 9 December 2018. Some statutes have been put away in special rooms. However, some offensive images are built in the walls, and it is said that these cannot be removed because heritage laws protect the building.[18] More recently, the San of South Africa fell victim to biopirating of the hoodia plant which they have been using for centuries to check hunger and thirst. This plant was patented by the Council for Scientific and Industrial Research (CSIR) of their government before licensing it to Phytopharm. Although through a claim the San will get a benefit from the CSIR royalties, the incident shows disregard for the knowledge and science of indigenous people.[19]

IV Solutions and Approaches to the Problem

After exposing some challenges and issues above, I would like now to present the following as solutions and approaches to dealing with what can be done to remove the persistence of colonialism in the way the West deals with non-Europeans in general, and from African technology in particular. The most general concern is anthropological since colonialism is grounded in how we conceive our relations to other people and nature. The full humanity and dignity of the African is not yet recognised. There are still racist ideologies and practices against the African in the Americas, Europe and even Russia. Legal, political and theological provisions can make a contribution, provided the victimiser does not dictate the undertaking. More initiatives should be taken by Africans, especially in the international fora, to promote respect for the African people. I am aware that this is not very simple because Africans themselves do contribute to their own humiliation and dehumanisation. Organisations and occasions which create occasions for African and Europeans to meet and interact as equals should be created or reinforced.

Education is an important tool in eliminating colonial mentalities. In this respect, academic programmes in the West and Africa need to be reviewed to eliminate traits discriminative ideologies and practices. The courses in science and history should be reviewed to include African science and technology. In the same vein, the epistemological question should be addressed to show that Africa has contributed and is contributing to the world scientific and technological patrimony.

On the theological level, the Church has a lot to do to rehabilitate its image with regard to how evangelisation promoted colonisation and dehumanisation of the African. There is need to use the same papal authority to revoke the bulls that justified and promoted colonisation and enslavement of the non-European people. Similarly, the Church's practices and teaching which are marked by Western universalising tendencies wrongly taken to be the teaching of the Church should be eliminated.

Notes

1. On this see Sandra Braman, 'Technology and Epistemology: Information Policy and Desire', in G. Bolin, Ed., *Cultural Technologies in Cultures of Technology: Culture as Means and Ends in a Technologically Advanced Media World*, New York: Routledge, 2012, pp. 133-150.
2. On this see, for example, Serena Tucci and Joshua M. Akey, 'Population Genetics: A Map of Human Wanderlust,' *Nature*, 538 no. 7624 (2016): 178-179
3. See https://en.wikipedia.org/wiki/Great_Sphinx_of_Giza
4. See https://www.youtube.com/watch?v=E3TQbV6cfQM
5. For examples of presentation on this see, with ample references, Wikipedia, History of science and technology in Africa, https://en.wikipedia.org/wiki/History_of_science_and_technology_in_Africa.
6. Ivan Van Sertima uses this title in the book, *Egypt: Child of Africa*, New Brunswick: Transaction Publishers, 2005. What was done and achieved in Egypt should be seen as African because of the influence of other African people, especially from along the Nile, on Egypt.
7. On this see Cheikh Anta Diop. *Civilization or Barbarism: An Authentic Anthropology*. New York: Lawrence Hill Books, 1991 and *The African Origin of Civilization: Myth or Reality*, New York: Lawrence Hill, 1974.
8. See Yosef A. A. ben-Jochannan, *Africa: Mother of Western Civlisation*, Baltimore: Black Classic Press, 1988.
9. See UNESCO, 'Annex to Chapter 1: Report of the Symposium on 'The Peopling of Ancient Egypt and the Deciphering of the Meroitic Script'', in G. Mokhtar, ed., *General History of Africa, Vol. II, Ancient Civilisations of Africa*, Berkeley: UNESCO, 1981, pp. 58-83.

10. On the genocide of the Aboriginals in the Australian sub-region, one can find sufficient bibliography in 'Colonial Genocides Project', on http://www.yale.edu/gsp/colonial/, on the massacres in the Americas, see David E. Stannard, *The American Holocaust: The Conquest of the New World*, New York: Oxford University Press, 1993, and on the massacres in the then Belgian Congo, see Adam Hochschild, *King Leopold's Ghost: A Story of Greed, Terror, and Heroism in Colonial Africa*, Boston: Houghton Mifflin Company, 1999 and of the Herero in Namibia, Reinhart Kössler and Henning Melber, The genocide in Namibia (1904-08) and its consequences in *Pambazuka News*, https://www.pambazuka.org, 20 March 2012.

11. The English text of *Dum diversas* is taken from http://unamsanctamcatholicam. blogspot.nl/2011/02/dum-diversas-english-translation.html, 5 February 2011

12. See Francis Gardiner Davenport (ed.), *European Treaties Bearing on the History of the United States and its Dependencies to 1648*, Washington, D. C.: Carnegie Institution of Washington, 1917, p. 9.

13. Ibid., p. 56.

14. One of the best presentations on this is by B.A. Hindsale, 'The Right of Discovery', in *Ohio Archaeological and Historical Quarterly*, 2/3 (1888) pp. 349-379.

15. For a more detailed discussion on *res nullus* see Hindsale, ibid., pp. 364-365.

16. Ibid., p. 365.

17. See *Le Point*, Un rapport sur la restitution d'oeuvres d'art à l'Afrique remis à Emmanuel Macron https://www.lepoint.fr/culture/un-rapport-sur-la-restitution-d-oeuvres-d-art-a-l-afrique-remis-a-emmanuel-macron-23-11-2018-2273753_3.php, 23 November 2018.

18. See Alex Marshall, Belgium's Africa Museum Had a Racist Image. Can It Change That?, *The New York Times*, 8 December 2018.

19. On this see Gavin Stenton, 'Biopiracy within Pharmaceutical Industry: A Stark Illustration of Just How Abusive, Manipulative and Perverse the Patenting Can Be towards Countries of the South', in *Hertfordshire Law Journal* 1/2 (2003), p. 33.) For more examples see, Jay McGown, *Out of Africa: Mysteries of Access and Benefit Sharing*, Washington: Edmonds Institute, 2006. See also Peter Kanyandago, 'Ecological and Ethical Implications of Pirating the Resources of Africa,' *Concilium* 51 no. 3 (2015): 89-95.

Technology and Cultural Values: Perspectives from India

KURUVILLA PANDIKATTU

The British Historian Arnold Toynbee claims that the 'Indian way' or 'an Indian ending' is the only way of salvation for humanity. This paper attempts to show that the Indian way is essentially a spiritual and philosophical way that is both rooted and open. Taking into account the present technological and cultural revolution, including the Fourth Industrial Revolution, the author pleads for a theology that responds critically and creatively to contemporary scientific revolution. Only by progressing technologically, ethically and spiritually can we flourish as human beings.

'The vast literature, the magnificent opulence, the majestic sciences, the soul touching music, the awe inspiring gods! It is already becoming clearer that a chapter which has a Western beginning will have to have an Indian ending if it is not to end in the self-destruction of the human race. At this supremely dangerous moment in history the only way of salvation for mankind is the Indian way. Here we have the attitude and spirit that can make it possible for the human race to grow together in to a single family,' claimed the British Historian Arnold Toynbee.[1] According to him, the 'Indian way' or 'an Indian ending' is the only way of salvation for humanity.[2] This paper attempts to explore this insight from our contemporary technological and cultural perspectives.

In recent years, India has witnessed extraordinary transformations not only in economic standards but also in sociocultural values. The traditional values, norms, and behaviours are being altered into more Westernised and global ones.[3] Indian youths may appear to endorse Western values, but family traditions, group values, and national traditions continue to play a pivotal role in determining brand meanings. So spirituality and religion continues to be central concerns even of the youth, who know that 'technology and innovation are at the heart of transforming India'.[4]

We base our exploration exclusively on five contemporary Indian thinkers. The first one by Nobel Laureate Amartya Sen, *The Argumentative Indian*, deals with democracy, development and by extension technology. Here, inspired by the argumentative culture of India, the author pleads for an egalitarian technological development in the context of globalization. The next thinker Shashi Tharoor,[5] former Undersecretary of United Nations, through his *The Elephant, The Tiger and the Cellphone*, takes us to the glorious and tolerant history of India.[6] The next author, the young and enterprising Chetan Bhagat, explores the agony and anxiety of the tech savvy youth in his *One night @ the call center*.[7]

Then we travel through the Fourth Industrial Revolution (FIR), which will drastically change Indian way of living, thinking and being through Pranjal Sharma's *Kranti Nation*.[8] Assuming that the Indian way or a story with an Indian ending is sustainable, we look into today's technological progress of the world. Then we hope to draw on the spiritual depth, typical of the Indian way, which alone can make contemporary world sustainable. So the challenge to theology is to enable a spirituality that is rooted and committed and at the same time creative and flexible to include all traditions and embrace diversities.

I Amartya Sen on Democracy, Development and Technology

In a marvellous collection of essays, Nobel laureate Amartya Sen smashes quite a few stereotypes and places the idea of India and Indianness in its rightful, deserved context.[9] Central to his notion of India, as the title, *The Argumentative Indian*, suggests, is the long tradition of argument and public debate, of intellectual pluralism and generosity that informs India's history.[10]

While talking about Indian democracy Amartya Sen is very clear: 'It is important to avoid the twin pitfalls of either taking democracy to be just

73

a gift of the Western world that India simply accepted when it became independent, or assuming that there is something unique in Indian history that makes the country singularly suited to democracy.'[11] The truth is far more complex and somewhere between these two views.

In this stirring book on the historical perceptions of India, Amartya Sen, gives his basic vision of India as:

India is an immensely diverse country with many distinct pursuits, vastly disparate convictions, widely divergent customs and a veritable feast of viewpoints. [Any talk about its history, culture or politics must] involve considerable selection ... the focus on the argumentative tradition in this work is also a result of choice. It does not reflect a belief that this is the only reasonable way of thinking about the history or culture or politics of India.[12]

In fact, the modern West, according to Sen, emphasized 'the differences – real or imagined – between India and the West,'[13] focusing on India's spiritual heritage at the expense of the rational one, partly because the West was naturally drawn to what was unique and different in India.

[Such] slanted emphases has tended to undermine an adequately pluralist understanding of Indian intellectual traditions. While India has ... a vast religious literature [with] grand speculation on transcendental issues ... there is also a huge – and often pioneering – literature, stretching over two and a half millennia, on mathematics, logic, epistemology, astronomy, physiology, linguistics, phonetics, economics, political science and psychology, among other subjects concerned with the here and now.[14]

And while India might offer 'examples of every conceivable type of attempt at the solution to the religious problem,' Sen submits that they 'coexist with deeply sceptical arguments ... (sometimes within the religious texts themselves).'[15] Among his examples is the 'song of creation' of the Rig Veda, 'the first extensive composition in any Indo-European language'[16] and the radical doubts expressed therein.

Both Sen and our next author give creative and diverse understandings of the Indian story, which is different from and related to the traditional outlook on Indian culture as religious, traditional and homogeneous.

II The Shashi Tharoor on Indian Tradition and Technology

Bewildering diversity is the very essence of India, observes novelist and former undersecretary of UN and career politician Shashi Tharoor the author of satirical novel *The Great Indian Novel*[17] in this engaging collection of essays, which tries to reconcile the country's clashing traditions with progress and liberalism. Hinduism's promiscuous openness to other beliefs and cultures makes it a model of secular tolerance, he argues. So Hindu fundamentalist bigotry is his favourite target.

Tharoor imagines that ancient Indian science had anticipated even quantum mechanics.[18] He celebrates India's compatibility with the global economy, a stance that occasionally shades into business promotion. In this book, the numerous articles portray quick, sketchy and creative picture takes on Indian cultural touchstones and developments. His sympathetic insight and incisive language combine in a fascinating portrait of Indian society.

He extols the virtues and spirit of Hinduism and the sense of plurality that it propagates. So we can appreciate his latest book, aptly titled *Why I am a Hindu*.[19] He adds how fundamentalism that divides people on the basis of religious and other identities, is in itself, against the principle of Hinduism. He affirms emphatically, 'No one identity can ever triumph in India; both the country's chronic plurality and the logic of the electoral market place make this impossible. India is never truer to itself than while celebrating its own diversity.'

III Chetan Bhagat on Call Centre Culture

Moving to contemporary technology, it may be noted that India succeeded phenomenally in two aspects: its successful and economic space programs and the software industry. Let me limit myself to the software industry here.

Signs of middle age were obvious at India's giant IT industry, which now has sales of $100 billion and is dominated by outsourcing firms. In one of their meetings held at a five-star hotel in Mumbai, the guests of honour were mostly politicians. They were accompanied by 'grey-haired, well-fed executives'. As *The Economist* points out it was difficult to spot anyone close to India's median age of 26.[20] Things have changed dramatically since 1981 when Infosys, the pioneering Indian IT firm, was founded in a flat by seven hungry and young engineers with mere $250 as investment.

India has already had one technology revolution. In the 1980s middle-class engineers from a dirt-poor India somehow persuaded Western firms to outsource their back-office functions and bits of their Information Technology (IT) operations to the subcontinent. Thus began a three-decade-long boom.

The revolution fed its children well. Thanks to IT, about three million Indians now work in well-paid formal jobs of the kind that India needs so badly. Perhaps another 10 million related have been created for maids, drivers and the like. Technology services have saved India from bankruptcy, keeping the balance of payments in adequate condition.[21] As well as local champions such as Infosys, TCS and Wipro, it is remarkable that 750 multinational firms have outsourcing and technology hubs in India, mainly performing research and development studies.

Until India became a technological super-power, technology was used mostly to increase production. India is probably the first country in the world to use technology to improve quality of life. We don't, therefore, have companies like Microsoft, Google, Apple and others, in India. Rather, India uses the resources that these big companies provide to improve quality of life in India, rather than evolving a 'broad based technological development'.[22]

The cultural impact of all this has been huge, as illustrated in best-selling novels of Chetan Bhagat. [23]

The story revolves around six people, three male and three female, only one of whom, the military uncle is elderly. All of them are working in a same group in a call centre. They all are different from each other but they have a similarity in them that all of them are fed up with their lives and their lives are very messy. This story is about a night at call centre which changes the lives of all the people, by changing their attitude. It changes their way to deal with the problems of their lives, by a call from God!

In short, the software industry provides India with a new opening. 'Many entrepreneurs are keen to address the opportunities and challenges that India offers.'[24]

IV Pranjal Sharma on Fourth Industrial Revolution

The Founder and Executive Chairman, World Economic Forum, Prof Klaus Schwab thinks that the world is on the verge of the Fourth Industrial Revolution 'that will fundamentally alter the way we live, work, and relate to one another. In its scale, scope, and complexity, the transformation will be unlike anything humankind has experienced before.'[25]

The fourth revolution can literally disrupt everything that we know today. Artificial intelligence, robotics, autonomous cars, advancement in biotech and genomics will all be part of the industrial revolution 4.0.[26]

Contrary to what the alleged ill-effects of the fourth revolution, the noted industrialist Baba Kalyani claims that 'India should benefit from it and there will be a spur in job creation.' He adds: 'India is in a very unique position to take advantage of the Fourth Industrial Revolution and do some amazing things that it had missed out on in the past.'[27]

When India changed its focus from cheap labour to a skilled workforce, technology and capital-intensive sectors, it became more competitive. Kalyani highlights: 'The lesson was very clear. We needed to move to an innovation-driven economy. The FIR provides us with a unique opportunity and knowledge base to move from a factor-driven to an innovation-driven economy.'[28]

Many economists are apprehensive of the FIR and its effect on job creation. According to some experts this revolution is likely 'to increase inequality in the world as the spread of machines increases markets and disrupts labor markets'.[29] More than 65% of India's workforce lives in rural areas, with relatively inadequate access to basic amenities. Water is scarce, sanitation is rudimentary, daily life is led through primitive means. Can this be addressed or at least enabled through initiatives under the FIR? Can such technology truly benefit us?[30]

It is in this context that we can appreciate Pranjal Sharma's book *Kranti Nation*.[31] The world is on the cusp of the 'Fourth Industrial Revolution,' he acknowledges. He records the positive transformation brought about by FIR and at the same time warns of grave job losses.

Kranti Nation − wherein KRANTI stands for knowledge, research and new technology: in Hindi the word 'kranti' means revolution − records the transformation that is taking place in 10 different sectors, including manufacturing, logistics, services, transportation, retail, mobility, healthcare, hospitality.[32]

Sharma, in fact, makes a strong point that automation may be highly beneficial for a country with sparse population but for India it might result in 1.5 million job losses a year.[33] That can cause serious economic and cultural upheaval, which must be factored in our plan for knowledge development.

V Drawing from the Wisdom of India

The scenario offered by FIR is mind-boggling. We are moving from reality to virtual reality. From life to artificial life. From carbon based body to silicon chips. From human beings to posthumans or extropians. The claim is made that we may eliminate death. Humans will become obsolete and Artificial intelligence and robotics may take over. It is in this context that we need to raise new philosophical and theological questions regarding our very existence. Can Indian story offer a way out?

Still we can ask the question: What makes up India and its rich culture? 'Outstanding Facts of Indian Culture' according to historian and statesman Sardar K.M. Panikkar[34] as:

1. Tradition of tolerance, aiding to the richness and variety of Indian life.
2. Sense of synthesis reflected in racial harmony, the primary institutions of the village and the family, sculpture, architecture, music and painting, modes of worship, faith in democratic institutions, etc.
3. Universal outlook as reflected in views such as 'The world is one family' and 'the world as one nest'.
4. Philosophical outlook with its basis in the belief in the unity of creation.
5. Respect for the individual based on the philosophical equation of Atman and Brahman, the soul and the Oversoul (Brahman).

Thus the Indian way or the Indian story may be summarized as follows: The spiritual or philosophical depth, together with an openness to the new and challenging, forms the essence of Indian culture, with its different colours, contradictions and diversity. Further deep spirituality and vibrant religiosity form the core of Indian ethos.

Given the history of 4000 years, we can believe that there is the inner resilience and sources of wisdom inherent in the Indian sources and traditions. Given the possibility that humans may merge with machines and nation states will merge with corporates, can they still live the 'Indian way?'

A culture that cherishes ambiguity, dances with diversity may be able to deal creatively with the coming revolution. A culture with is profoundly complex and subtle can choose from the various possibilities. A culture which is primarily spiritual (without denying this worldly dimensions of it) may be able to flourish in the uncertainty, ambiguity and possibility emerging from the FIR.

A culture that has given birth to Buddha, Ashoka and Gandhi and four living religions will be able to find meaning in the uncertainties of the immediate future. We need a holistic and integrated approach,[35] fostering capabilities of human beings.[36]

Looking at FIR only from ethical or social perspectives, though praiseworthy, is not sufficient. Given the way FIR is going to alter the manner we think, we act and we are, we need to formulate a creative critique of it that considers the anthropological, ecological and theological dimensions of this technology. Thus, the only way humanity can celebrate life and survive harmoniously is if we can make Indian way, that of the whole world: an inclusive, integrated, holistic and spiritual way!

VI Conclusion

Thus the challenge to thinkers, philosophers and theologians is to usher in a deep spirituality that can dialogue with contemporary FIR, guide it critically and creatively forward and make our lives more fulfilling. We need to draw from the various (even conflicting) sources of wisdom!

Notes

1. Toynbee, Arnold. *One World and India,* New Delhi: Indian Council for Cultural Relations, 1960. 54.
2. Pandikattu, Kuruvilla, *An Indian Ending: Rediscovering the Grandeur of Indian Heritage for a Sustainable Future*, New Delhi: Serials Publications, 2013.
3. See Schaniel, William C. 'New Technology and Culture Change in Traditional Societies' *Journal of Economic Issues*, Vol. 22, No. 2 (Jun., 1988), pp. 493-498. Accessed at https://www.jstor.org/stable/4226008 on July 3, 2018.
4. Kant, Amitabh 'In an Innovation Nation,' *Economic Times*, November 25, 2018. Accessed at https://economictimes.indiatimes.com/blogs/et-commentary/in-an-innovation-nation/ on July 23, 2018. See also Pandikattu, Kuruvilla. (2003) 'The Indian Paradox: Scientifically Foreword, Religiously Inward and Economically Backward.' In: Pandikattu, K., Vonach, A. (eds) *Religion, Society and Economy*. Frankfurt am Main: Peter Lang, pp. 133-148.
5. Tharoor, Shashi, *The Elephant, the Tiger & the Cellphone: India, the Emerging 21st-Century Power*, Penguin Viking, 2007.
6. Adiga, Aravind. *The White Tiger*. London: Atlantic Books, 2008.
7. Bhagat, Chetan. *One Night at the Call Centre*. London: Black Swan, 2012.
8. Sharma, Pranjal, *Kranti Nation: India and the Fourth Industrial Revolution*. New Delhi: Macmillan, 2017.
9. Sen, Amartya. *The Argumentative Indian: Writings on Indian Culture, History and Identity*, London: Allen Lane, 2005.
10. Bhattacharya, Soumya (2005) 'Beyond the Call Centre' *The Guardian*, Sun 3 Jul 2005. Accessed at https://www.theguardian.com/books/2005/jul/03/historybooks.features on November 2, 2018.
11. Sen, 2005, 13.
12. Sen, 2005, ix.
13. Sen, 2005, 23.
14. Sen 2005, 159.
15. Sen 2005, xi.
16. Wendy Doniger, *The Rig Veda*, London, Penguin, 2005.
17. Tharoor, Shashi. *The Great Indian Novel*. Haryana: Penguin, 2014.
18. Rao, J. S. 'Science and Technology in India.' *Science, New Series*, Vol. 229, No. 4709 (Jul. 12, 1985), p. 130.
19. Tharoor, Shashi. *Why I Am a Hindu*. London: Hurst & Company 2018.
20. The Screen Revolution (2013), *The Economist*, March 16, 2013, https://www.economist.com/business/2013/03/16/the-screen-revolution, accessed on March 3, 2018
21. Ibid.
22. Kumar. Duru Arun (2012). 'Technology Growth in India – Some Important Concerns,' *Polish Sociological Review*, No. 178 (2012), pp. 295-302. https://www.jstor.org/stable/41969446
23. Bhagat, 2012.
24. Kant 2018.
25. Schwab, Klaus, 'The Fourth Industrial Revolution: what it means, how to respond,' *World Economic Forum*, 2016, accessed at https://www.weforum.org/agenda/2016/01/the-fourth-industrial-revolution-what-it-means-and-how-to-respond/14 Jan 2016, on Nov 2, 2018.

26. Worldfolio, 'The Fourth Industrial Revolution and its impact on India's job creation and skills enhancement,' 2015, accessed at http://www.theworldfolio.com/news/the-fourth-industrial-revolution-and-its-impact-on-indias-job-creation-and-skills-enhancement/4083/ on Sept 4, 2018.

27. Ibid.

28. Ibid.

29. Ibid.

30. Tan, Teck-Boon and Wu Shang-su, 'Public Policy Implications of the Fourth Industrial Revolution for Singapore: Coping with an Uncertain Future,' *S. Rajaratnam School of International Studies* (2017) accessed at https://www.jstor.org/stable/resrep17650.7 on July 3, 2018.

31. Sharma, 2017.

32. Panda, Subrata, 'How the Fourth Industrial Revolution Can Make or Mar India's Fortunes,' *The Print*, 2018, https://theprint.in/pageturner/afterword/industrial-revolution-india-kranti-nation-review/47789/ 8 April, 2018. Accessed on August 2018.

33. Ibid.

34. Panikkar, K. M. *A Survey of Indian History*. London: Asia Publishing House, 1971, 2-3.

35. Malik, S.C. 'Science, Technology and Culture: A Holistic Approach,' *Indian Anthropologist*, Vol. 27, No. 2 (December, 1997), pp. 1-17.

36. Sen, Amartya. *Employment, Technology, and Development*. Oxford: Clare

Part Three: Technology in the Service of Humanity

Technology in the Service of Humanity: Perspectives on Gender and Inclusion

SHARON A. BONG

This paper calls to question not only how we understand our place in this world but also what it means to be human in relation to other humans, other species and the environment at large. The paper traces ontological and theological shifts through the trope of the womb as cosmic, material, and virtual sites of contestation: firstly, through the centring of the human in creation based on the Pope's encyclical Laudato Si'*; and secondly, the decentring of the human in creation through reproductive technologies, e.g. artificial wombs and its implications for the unborn, women, pregnant (trans)men.*

Technology that matters is technology that serves humanity. Technology that is in the service of humanity is grounded in a Christian world-view that cements the place of humans in the world. Are these truth claims universally acknowledged? How would these truth claims hold up when appraised from a feminist lens that privileges gender diversity and inclusion of not only humans but also other species that are connected to humanity as a biological community?

This paper aims to offer a theological reflection on the question of gender and inclusion with a focus on reproductive technologies that are in the service of humanity paradoxically in calling to question not only how we understand our place in this world but also what it means to be human in relation to other humans, other species and the environment at large.

The paper traces ontological and theological shifts through the trope of the womb as cosmic, material, and virtual sites of contestation: firstly, through the centring of the human in creation based on the Pope's encyclical *Laudato Si'* (hereafter LS) manifested in technologies of, for and by humans;[1] and secondly, the decentering of the human in creation through reproductive technologies, e.g. artificial wombs and its implications for the unborn, women, pregnant (trans)men. The paper argues for a decentring of the human in creation and concomitant foregrounding of radical relationality between humans and other species, to better embrace the sacredness of all in creation, in this Anthropocene Age of ecological crises that is culpably impacted by humans. The ways in which this endeavour – a feminist theoretical, theological and political praxis – potentially engenders post-gender, post-Christian, and post-human considerations, will now be borne.

I Centring of the human in creation

The parameters that govern technology's service to humanity are expounded in LS, a faith-based text that contemporaneously and urgently exhorts an 'ecological conversion' (LS, 217) in aspiring towards climate justice, consonant with the United Nations' globally-endorsed Sustainable Development Goals. The integrity of technologies of, for and by humans are juxtaposed against the sacredness of creation of the Originator of Life: 'How wonderful is the certainty that each human life is not adrift in the midst of hopeless chaos, in a world ruled by pure chance or endlessly recurring cycles! The Creator can say to each one of us: 'Before I formed you in the womb, I knew you' (Jer 1.5). We were conceived in the heart of God' (LS, 65). The trope of the cosmic womb is metaphorical; it signifies Nature – of which the woman's uterus is a microcosmic version of – and the omniscience of its 'Creator', God the Father. The binary between order/chaos is established, with the purposeful not randomised inception of 'each human life', and this binary is further gender scripted through the matrimonial union of man and his wife in begetting life which in turn, renders the human as agentic participants in the 'recurring cycles' of life on earth.[2]

Knowing one's place in the world is keeping to one's place in the world: as the Creator God and His creations are mutually exclusive categories; the human may seek to imitate but may not exceed his/her God-given talents in appropriating the Source of Life. When 'the harmony between the Creator, humanity and creation as a whole was disrupted by [the human] presuming to take the place of God and refusing to acknowledge our creaturely limitations,' this 'rupture is sin' (LS, 66). The first governing principle of the Christian world-view is thus a hierarchical ordering of Creator/creation; God/nature (comprising human, non-human and other species).

Ensuing from the hierarchical ordering of creation is the second governing principle which is anthropocentrism; the centring of the human above non-human and other species in creation. The human is conferred 'an infinite dignity', literally stands above non-humans and other species as the human alone is created in 'God's image and likeness' (LS, 65) and has the unique capacity to reason (LS, 81). The hierarchically-ordered relationship of God/human/nature (comprising non-human and other species), as opposed to 'a world ruled by pure chance or endlessly recurring cycles', renders morally acceptable, experimentation on animals for the sake of 'saving human lives' (LS, 130) but not 'living human embryos' (LS, 136). The primacy of the human and concomitant utility value of non-human and other species as objects of human-driven scientific endeavours is inferred as 'human beings [possess] a particular dignity above other creatures' (119). Ontologically, not all are created equal.

Flowing from both these fundamental principles is the third principle that is related to the excesses of anthropocentrism framed within a 'technocratic paradigm' that is *undifferentiated and one-dimensional*' that is largely blamed for the ecological crises today (LS, 106). The Church as the first violator, holds itself accountable, for its once 'mistaken understanding of [its] own principles has at times led [it] to justify mistreating nature, to exercise tyranny over creation' (LS, 200). It now accountably advocates for 'responsible stewardship' (LS, 116). In doing so, the Church adroitly positions not anthropocentrism in and of itself as problematic but rather, its excesses manifested in at least two ways. In the first instance, there is 'modern (secularized) anthropocentrism' where 'the technological mind sees nature as an insensate order, as a cold body of facts, as a mere 'given', as an object of utility' which compromises 'the (biblically-supported) intrinsic dignity of the world' and all that inhabit it (LS, 115). It is further denounced as 'a tyrannical anthropocentrism' that does not 'respect the laws of nature and the delicate equilibria existing between the creatures of this world' (LS, 68); an 'equilibra' that rests on the hierarchical ordering of God/human/nature. Essentially, 'dominion' over non-human and other species is in keeping with God's plan but not '*absolute* dominion over other creatures' (LS, 67, italics mine).

Is it then surprising that the other instance of excessive anthropomorphism that veers from this divine plan, what LS terms as a 'misguided anthropocentrism,' is 'biocentrism'; where 'the human person is considered as simply one being among others' (LS, 118), i.e. not centred in creation above non-human and other species. Such a standpoint coheres with queer ecofeminism that embraces the inherent dignity of all – human, non-human and other species (e.g. advocating for animal rights on par with human rights)³ – and draws a parallelism between gender diversity and inclusion (of the entire spectrum of human sexuality) and biological diversity (biodiversity).⁴ I argue that such a standpoint more faithfully coheres with a relationality that is founded on inclusiveness, interdependency and mutuality which is what LS ambivalently exhorts; 'When we fail to acknowledge as part of reality the worth of a poor person, a human embryo, a person with disabilities – to offer just a few examples – it becomes difficult to hear the cry of nature itself; everything is connected' (LS, 117). Connectivity however, within a Christian world-view, has its limits, given its anthropocentric base and bias.

As such, the parameters that govern technology's service to humanity as expounded in LS present a Christian world-view that denotes sinful 'rupture' firstly, as human hubris in overreaching his/her potential, for instance, to advance life-giving or life-taking reproductive technologies and secondly, a 'tyrannical anthropocentrism' that is 'unconcerned for other creatures' (LS, 68). On the first point, humans 'have the freedom needed to limit and direct technology' which includes experimentation on non-human and other species for the sake of the human; 'primarily to resolving people's concrete problems, truly helping them live with more dignity and less suffering' (LS, 112).

On the second point, there is no 'justification of abortion' as it is 'incompatible with the protection of nature' that begins with the protection of the (human) embryo given the interrelatedness of all creation (LS, 120). Abortion and by extension, 'certain politics of 'reproductive health'' aimed at global overpopulation (LS, 50) are branded as weak responses to the cries of the (feminized) earth. And the scourge of any technology that is aimed at reducing the 'presence of human beings' (LS, 60), created *imago dei* and conferred 'a particular dignity above other creatures' (119), is as culpable as systemic violations of climate and social justice such as 'ecological debt' between the global north and south (LS, 51), 'techno-economic paradigm' (LS, 53), a 'deified market' (LS, 56), 'self-interested pragmatism' and 'the paradigm of consumerism' (LS, 215). With an illusion to the 'politics of reproductive technology'[5] that throws into relief, uterus wars – that pit a woman's choice to self-determination and bodily integrity against the weight of biological, national, cultural imperatives of motherhood and the ensuing ethical burden these have on women whose bodies are differently marked by age, class, ethnicity, religiosity – women's voices and lived experiences are, in one fell swoop, elided. Ultimately, reproductive technologies that are accorded legitimacy are those that embrace the 'culture of life' (with the heterosexual family at its heart) and reject the 'culture of death' (LS, 213).

II De-centring of the human in creation

Yet how would the parameters that govern technology's service to humanity that are informed by a Christian world-view as elucidated above, be brought to bear on the phenomenon of artificial wombs that arguably embraces the 'culture of life' (LS, 213)? Would similar legitimacy be accorded to artificial wombs, when one weighs the biotechnological breakthrough in light of ethical implications for the unborn, women who signify both a real and *potentially* 'maternal body',[6] transwomen who desire to mother and pregnant (trans)men who do? Artificial wombs call to question not only sex/gender binaries that frame the human person in aligning the maternal body with (natural) womanhood but also what it fundamentally means to be human where being naturally human, created *imago dei*, is predicated on fixed biological and ontological differences. The womb becomes a highly emotive site of contestation embroiled not only in the 'politics of reproductive technology'[7] but also 'fetal politics' that pit the rights of the unborn (elevated to the status of personhood) against the rights of the pregnant woman (dehumanized as a vessel for the unborn and her pregnancy, medicalized although it is not an illness and managed, professionally and often intrusively).[8]

Ectogenesis or the 'invention of a complete external womb' or 'baby pouch'[9] may be the stuff that science-fiction (notably, genetically modified, hierarchically-ordered humans decanted from artificial wombs in Huxley's *Brave New World*) is made of but a biotechnological breakthrough spells miracle, hope or doom depending on one's unmet need and political and religious ideologies. In April 2017, at the Children's Hospital of Philadelphia, lamb foetuses at the equivalent of a premature human foetus of 22-24 weeks were 'able to successfully grow in the biobag, with the oldest lamb now more than one year old'.[10] The 'transparent, womb-like vessels' in which the lamb foetuses floated in for 'four weeks after birth', a 'pioneering approach' from conventional incubators 'could act as an urgently needed bridge between the mother's womb and the outside world for babies born at between 23-28 weeks gestation'.[11] The 'limit of viability for premature babies has been steadily pushed back to about 23 weeks' as a result of previous biotechnological breakthroughs in the past decade.[12] Where critically premature babies are by nature just 'not ready' to be outside their mothers' wombs, a simulated womb affords that less-than-natural albeit critical bridge between life and death by following through the gestation period.

Related biotechnological breakthroughs include human embryos kept alive 'outside the body for 13 days using a mix of nutrients that mimic conditions in the womb'.[13] Scientists believe that narrowing the gap between the 'longest time embryos can survive and the earliest time a foetus is viable (i.e. can survive)' will facilitate the technology for ectogenesis. The benefits of ectogenesis or artificial wombs include increasing the survival rates of critically premature babies, and fertility options not only for the infertile, those past reproductive age but also those who fall outside the natural (heterosexual) family, e.g. homosexual and transgender parenting.

Today, experimentation on 'spare, donated IVF embryos' is governed by a legal rather than scientific limit that is likely to be reviewed, as the '14-day stage marks the point when the individuality of an embryo is assured, because they can no longer split into twins'.[14] 'Womb transplantation' already a reality for women since 2014 (with five babies successfully born) – as many women are born 'without a womb, and others are forced to have theirs removed due to cancer and other conditions' – could be extended and as some would posit, should be extended on the basis of equality, for 'transwomen who are going to want a uterus'.[15] In July 2017, a British transmen 'put a full sex change (sex reassignment surgery) on hold' to give birth to a baby girl.[16]

The reality of artificial wombs that proliferates and diversifies vessels of life, e.g. incubators, biobags and womb transplants, has obvious theological and gendered implications. Theologically, the first principle of parameters that govern technology's service to humanity, the hierarchical ordering of God/human/nature, is transgressed: 'Once the human being declares independence from reality and behaves with absolute dominion, the very foundations of our life begin to crumble, for 'instead of carrying out his role as a cooperator with God in the work of creation, man sets himself up in place of God and thus ends up provoking a rebellion on the part of nature" (LS, 117). The human exceeds 'his role as a cooperator with God in the work of creation': the human becomes a co-creator of reproductive technologies that embrace the 'culture of life' by eschewing the 'culture of death' in sustaining the lives of critically premature babies or giving hope of nurturing life to those who are made worthy because they desire it (LS, 213). The second principle of anthropocentrism is similarly unsettled as the extension of life of the human is based on experimentation not only of the foetus of other species (e.g. lambs which is reminiscent of the Lamb of God) but also 'living human embryos': 'There is a tendency to justify transgressing all boundaries when experimentation is carried out on living human embryos. We forget that the inalienable worth of a human being transcends his or her degree of development' (LS, 136). It finally manifests as 'misguided anthropocentrism,' in the form of 'biocentrism'; where 'the human person is considered as simply one being among others' (LS, 118) as 'spare, donated IVF embryos' like the foetuses of lambs have 'inalienable worth' in advancing life-giving biotechnologies.

From a gendered lens, artificial wombs firstly challenge 'biological and repronormative discourses – those which materialize and maternalize female identity'.[17] On the one hand, some feminists 'construct pregnancy discrimination as sex discrimination' in the interests of (biological) women to claim an identity politics that aligns potential motherhood with womanhood.[18] This political standpoint inadvertently discriminates against pregnant men and transgender persons who may, as a consequence, be denied their reproductive rights. In this regard, the biological determinism of sex/gender binaries which are consonant with laws of (God-given) nature is maintained. Reproductive technologies disrupt such neat alignments of 'sex, gender identity and identification as mother/father' through the materialization and maternalization of men who have wombs and who desire to mother.[19]

On the other hand, artificial wombs potentially compound the objectification even dehumanization of pregnant women in contrast to the fetal subject that achieves personhood status as a 'child-to-be'.[20] 'Fetal politics' that encompass the rituals of prenatal care which a responsible mother-to-be would subject herself to involve disembodiment (as she surrenders her autonomy and first-hand experience of pregnancy) and dependency on experts (as her pregnancy is medicalized and subjected to the surveillance of professionals, and the ubiquitous obstetrical ultrasound). The pregnant woman is almost infantilized as she is made to 'doubt her own corporeality' by ascribing to herself 'developmental stages, risk figures, and hormone levels – technological abstractions that she is supposed to consider more real than what she feels and can see with her own eyes'.[21] The foetus that the pregnant woman experiences as it is mediated via the machine becomes a 'cyborg foetus' and her womb rendered virtual given her disassociation with it through the technologization of her material condition.[22]

The cyborg, to conclude, as conceived by Donna Harraway, is 'a creature in a post-gender world...[it] is resolutely committed to partiality, irony, intimacy, and perversity. It is oppositional, utopian, and completely without innocence'.[23] It engenders 'three crucial boundary breakdowns': human and animal,[24] animal-human (organism) and machine[25] and physical and non-physical.[26] The cyborg, potentially births post-gender, post-Christian, and post-human dilemmas in dismantling sex/gender boundaries that form what is fundamentally human into a work-in-progress, stretches the relationality between human and other species and in doing so, de-centres the human in creation. The hierarchical ordering of God/human/nature is potentially dislocated and relocated through the trope of the womb; at once, cosmic, material and virtual. Reproductive technologies when appraised from a feminist theoretical, theological and political praxis serve humanity by affirming the diversity and inclusion of the human, non-human and other species, locatable as a mutually-constituted biological community.

Notes

1. Pope Francis, 'Encyclical Letter Laudato Si' of the Holy Father Francis on Care for Our Common Home', 24 May 2015 at: http://w2.vatican.va/content/francesco/en/encyclicals/documents/papa-francesco_20150524_enciclica-laudato-si.html
2. For a fuller gendered analysis of LS, see Sharon A. Bong, 'Not Only For the Sake of Man: Asian Feminist Theological Responses to Laudato Si', in G. J.-S. Kim and H. P. Koster (eds), *Planetary Solidarity: Global Women's Voices on Christian Doctrine and Climate Justice*, Minneapolis: Fortress Press, 2017, pp. 81-96.
3. For a counter-argument on animal rights, see D. Slicer, 'Your Daughter or your Dog? A Feminist Assessment of the Animal Research Issue', *Hypatia*, 6, 1 (Spring, 1991), 108–24.
4. See C. J. Adams, 'Ecofeminism and the Eating of Animals', *Hypatia*, 6, 1 (Spring, 1991), 125-145 who argues for a more inclusive ecofeminist discourse that accords equal important to the 'domination of animals' as it does, the 'domination of nature'.
5. J. Wajcman, *Feminism Confronts Technology*, Cambridge: Polity Press, 1991, p. 62.
6. A. Balsamo, *Technologies of the Gendered Body: Reading Cyborg Women*, Durham and London: Duke University, 1999, Press, p. 90.
7. Wajcman, *Feminism Confronts Technology*, p. 62.
8. S. Samerski, 'Pregnancy, personhood, and the making of the fetus', in L. Disch and M. Hawkesworth (eds), *The Oxford Handbook of Feminist Theory*, New York: Oxford University Press, 2016, p. 700.
9. H. Sedgwick, 'Artificial Wombs Could Soon Be a Reality. What Will this Mean for Women?', *The Guardian*, 4 September 2017 at: https://www.theguardian.com/lifeandstyle/2017/sep/04/artifical-womb-women-ectogenesis-baby-fertility
10. Ibid.
11. H. Devlin, 'Artificial Wombs for Premature Babies Successful in Animal Trials', *The Guardian*, 25 April 2017 at: https://www.theguardian.com/science/2017/apr/25/artificial-womb-for-premature-babies-successful-in-animal-trials-biobag
12. Ibid.
13. Sedgwick, 'Artificial Wombs Could Soon Be a Reality'.
14. I. Sample, 'Researchers Break Record for Keeping Lab-Grown Human Embryos Alive', *The Guardian*, 5 May 2016 at: https://www.theguardian.com/science/2016/may/04/scientists-break-record-for-keeping-lab-grown-human-embryos-alive
15. H. Bodkin, 'Sex-Change Men 'Will Soon Be Able to Have Babies'', *The Telegraph*, 4 November 2017 at: https://www.telegraph.co.uk/news/2017/11/04/babies-born-transgender-mothers-could-happen-tomorrow-fertility/
16. Ibid.
17. L. Karaian, 'Pregnant Men: Repronormativity, Critical Trans Theory and Re(Conceive)ing of Sex and Pregnancy in Law', *Social & Legal Studies*, 22, 2 (2013), 211.

18. Ibid.
19. Ibid., 213.
20. Samerski, 'Pregnancy, personhood, and the making of the fetus', p. 707.
21. Ibid, p. 703.
22. Ibid.
23. D. J. Haraway, 'A Cyborg Manifesto: Science, Technology, and Socialist-Feminism in the Late Twentieth Century', in *Simians, Cyborgs, and Women: The Reinvention of Nature*, New York and London: Routledge, 1991, pp. 150–151.
24. Ibid., pp. 151–152.
25. Ibid., pp. 152–153.
26. Ibid., pp. 153–154.

Responsibility – Old or New?: Reflections on the Pros and Cons of a Transformation of Responsibility

JANINA LOH

On all sides there are expressions of concern that as a result of current challenges from digitalisation and automation in our modern, technology-based mass society, final limits are being set to responsibility. How can there be responsibility in the global financial market system, where algorithms operate that not even any longer understood by those who have programmed them (at least that is what they claim), or with responsibility as regards autonomous driver assistance systems? Despite this the call for responsibility seems to have lost none of its vehemence. This article offers some reflections on how we can deal with the fact that we are clearly struggling with responsibility.

We live in a time of strong concepts. For example, it is assumed that *fundamental upheavals* are taking place in human nature as a result of the development of autonomous artificial systems capable of independent learning. It will be possible, we are told, for human beings to be combined with machines and very soon for their minds to be uploaded on to a computer in order to escape the fragile, mortal husk that is their body. There is talk of a radical paradigm shift in the way our social, political and economic systems are organised as a result of the challenges of automation, digitalisation and Industry 4.0. There is a fear that machines will take over our work and so rob human beings of the basis for their existence, their social recognition and what makes their lives worth living. Others prophesy a *revolution in our perception of time and space* from modern information and communication technologies and the development of virtual reality. According to the specialist in the ethics of information, the Italian Luciano Floridi, the so-called Generation Z (those born after the year 2000) the hyper-historical age is dawning, since with this generation the boundary between online and offline will finally disappear completely. From the moment they open their eyes, the world this Generation Z encounters is wireless; they are not only permanently online but totally *onlife*. People of this generation lead a life online and have an online identity. They are *inforgs*, Floridi's coinage for a blend of 'informational' and 'organism'.[1] Much is also asked of the idea of transformation: everything will be transformed: our living spaces, cities and road networks by the introduction of autonomous driver assistance systems, the educational system in order to adapt it to the new political and economic conditions, and finally human beings themselves through technological changes and finally by being introduced into the domain of the virtual by mind-uploading to a post-human creature.[2] Does this also transform their responsibility?

On all sides concern is expressed that, as a result of the situations described and others in our modern, technology-dominated mass society, final limits are being set to responsibility, even dangerous holes are appearing in our possibilities for attributing responsibility that deepen into abysses that in the end irrevocably swallow our conventional understanding of responsibility. Nonetheless the call for responsibility is also losing none of its force. This article offers some suggestions on how to deal with the fact that we are obviously struggling with responsibility.

Responsibility is traditionally seen analytically as an individual phenomenon, that is, in the original understanding of the word there must be a single person to whom responsibility can be attributed. Responsibility in the classical sense is borne or held by someone. The noun first appears in English in the 18th century, but the adjective 'responsible' is recorded in the previous century. Responsibility may be held for an object, and a person may be responsible to a body or an interested party on criteria applying specifically to this context. For example, a thief is responsible for a theft (the action and the object stolen) before a court (authority) and to the person who has been robbed (interested party) on the basis of criteria embodied in law. This example shows that responsibility – and this is also implied by the etymology[3] – brings together (1) the ability to answer for something in terms of rules (2) and (3) a specific psychological make-up that makes a person responsible. I call this the minimal definition of responsibility. The person responsible feels (3.1) addressed and affected. He or she can understand the responsibility because they (3.2) are endowed with specific cognitive abilities and as a result of a process of reflection (3.3) adopt an attitude that corresponds to the significance of responsibility. The third component of the minimal definition in particular makes clear that responsibility demands more than simply giving an answer, and this is given expression in the seriousness and awareness of the responsible person, again reflected etymologically in the expression 'to answer for something'. It follows from this that the person on whom responsibility is to be laid is considered to have specific competences that enable him or her to take responsibility; these might be the ability to communicate and act, or autonomy and judgment.[4]

The transfer of responsibility to groups has, logically, brought up the question of the situation of the individuals and their individual responsibility within the collective body: is it just as large (quantitatively) and is it still 'the same' (qualitatively) as outside the group? Do all the members of a group still have 'full' responsibility for the matter in question, or merely partial responsibility? Legally the challenge of attributing collective responsibility was dealt with through a distinction between a natural person and a legal entity. In the end, however, here too the responsibility is taken back to the individuals involved and their roles and functions within the group, and individual responsibility in each case defined on that basis.

In analysis of responsibility a distinction is made between 'reductionism or ethical individualism' and 'collectivism and corporativism'.[5] Reductionism has no time for collective responsibility, and regards it as an empty phrase, since in the true sense individual responsibility is the only responsibility that exists. Indeed, a radical reductionist would argue, the concept of collective responsibility should be deleted from our vocabulary, since there is no significant distinction between genuine individual responsibility and responsibility as a member of a group. They might, for example, argue that 'Every group member is 'fully' responsible,' or 'Every group member is 'partially' responsible.'[6] Collectivism, on the other hand, starts from the premise that collective responsibility can acquire an autonomous status as opposed to individual mechanisms of attributing responsibility. A radical collectivist assumes that a collective responsibility exists without individual responsibility on the part of the group in question in that 'the group as such is fully...and exclusively responsible, that is, that no member of the group is responsible'. A hybrid approach, which attempts to steer a middle course between radical reductionism and radical collectivism, includes the positions that 'the group as such... and all its members are fully responsible,' and equally that 'the group as such... is fully responsible and all the members... are partially responsible.'

This short survey indicates that the step from a belief in clear individual responsibility to a position of trans-individual responsibility confronts us with enormous challenges in view of the number (quantitative) and nature (qualitative) of cases of responsibility in question. What happens when someone is a member of a group, but had absolutely no personal involvement in the circumstances of which the group is held responsible? Or, even more irritating, what about contexts in which it seems that absolutely no-one can be held responsible for what has happened? Since the 20th century human beings have increasingly operated in such untransparent relationships that Hans Jonas at an early stage responded in his book *The Imperative of Responsibility* with reflections on a new categorical imperative (drawing on Immanuel Kant's idea). What is the situation, for example, with responsibility for the climate, with responsibility in the global financial market system, where algorithms operate that even those who wrote them no longer understand (at least so they claim) or with responsibility in dealing with autonomous driver assistance systems?[7]

For such cases, in which responsibility ought to be attributed, but the subject position of the responsibility in question apparently cannot be filled, some responsibility theorists in recent years have attempted to develop helpful provisional concepts that manage without defining this term. For example, there is the term 'system responsibility', which is intended to mean that 'the system' is responsible while the individual members of the system have no responsibility. Positions like this are radical versions of the collectivism we looked at earlier. I am extremely sceptical about the value of such approaches. In the end, in practice we always look for a person or persons who is in a position to bear the alleged responsibility. Our understanding of responsibility traditionally works in this way. But if we abandon this, how should we proceed in such contexts?

In general, we seem to have two possible ways to restoring the credibility of responsibility. On the one hand we could try to renew the conventional individual understanding of responsibility so as to be able to carry on talking about responsibility in the usual sense without falling into the trap of a radical collectivism or fall victim to misleading ideas of system responsibility. To do this I should like to adopt Christian Neuhäuser's concept responsibility networks and give it more focus.[8] At the same time we could act on an appeal for a transformation of the traditional concept of responsibility, for example, by reviewing Neuhäuser's five items, modifying elements of the minimal definition mentioned above, or even our varying ideas about the subject of responsibility. Examples of these approaches are to be found in Hannah Arendt, Donna Haraway, Rosi Braidotti and Karen Barad, though there is no room here for a more detailed discussion.

The view underlying my ideas and an expansion of Neuhäuser's concept of responsibility networks is that we attribute responsibility to all the parties in a given situation who are involved in the event in question to the degree that they have the necessary abilities to allow us to attribute responsibility to them. To keep to the example of autonomous driver assistance systems mentioned previously, the responsibility network 'responsibility in traffic' should include first automatic cars and the human drivers (even if they are not actively involved in the driving process), the owners, the sellers, programmers, designers, the public, lawyers, driving instructors – in short all those involved in traffic.

Responsibility networks are unusually wide and include within them a variety of objects of responsibility. The term 'responsibility networks' can be used when one really no longer knows – and these are the sort of contexts we are talking about – whether the concept of responsibility can be given any meaningful content, precisely because, for example, it is difficult to determine the subject, no clear authority can be identified or the rules governing the situation cannot be specified. In a responsibility network the parties involved have different functions or occupy several positions at the same time: at one time they may be the subjects, at another the authorities and in yet another case the object and perhaps the same time the injured party where there is a question of responsibility.

It would be extremely difficult to identify one or several specific subjects of responsibility for 'responsibility in traffic' because the situation is far too broad for one person or a small number of individuals to be answerable. As a responsibility network, 'responsibility in traffic' encompasses several areas, for example, moral, legal and political responsibilities (defined by moral, legal and political rules). Traffic is the overall object of responsibility, though there is not one or several people who can sensibly said to have overall responsibility for it, since it divides into various less complex objects for which various parties take a specific responsibility. Responsibility for traffic can in one case mean the safety of the people involved in traffic, in another understanding responsibility for efficiently getting from A to B and in yet another case responsibility for ensuring that the moral challenges that go with participation in traffic have been made clear in advance to those involved in traffic. On the objects of partial responsibility mentioned (and various others), it can already be seen that in each case we are inclined to identify quite different subjects as assuming responsibility in different degrees, since there are always different authorities, interested parties and rules, and all require their specific responsibility in each case to be defined.

Currently an autonomous driver assistance system, which can only in a very weak sense – if at all – be identified as a responsible actor, because it lacks the relevant competences (ability to communicate and ability to act, as well as autonomous judgment), will not be able to occupy the position of subject of a responsibility within the responsibility network 'responsibility in traffic'. There are always potentially better qualified bearers of responsibility. Nonetheless it is conceivable to integrate it into one or more of the responsibilities of this responsibility network.

In this way responsibility can still be defined even in non-transparent contexts in which, for example, because of the algorithms and robots involved it may initially seem that a clear identification of responsible subjects would be difficult. Perhaps, therefore, we have no need to transform our traditional understanding of responsibility but merely change the interpretive level in cases where the frame of reference – as in the example we discussed of 'responsibility in traffic' – seems too broad, to a level that enables us to correlate different responsibilities each with its own subject and object of responsibility, relevant authorities, interested parties and applicable criteria.

On the other hand, this approach perhaps does not do justice to the new demands of the age of automation, digitalisation, Industry 4.0 and globally networked technologies.[9] Perhaps it is time for a radical review of the humanistic image underlying our conventional understanding of responsibility, namely that of a self-sufficient, sovereign individual endowed with various strong competences such as autonomy, ability to act and judgment. Now at last its inadequacies are becoming obvious, since it is these that have led us to this point of considering whether attribution of responsibility is any longer possible in the same way in an age of autonomous algorithms. Another consideration is that humanism, in its overwhelming concentration on the Western, white, version of humanity, as a result operates with an exclusive, anthropocentric and species-ist anthropology that tends morally to downgrade human beings that deviate from the 'norm' and discriminate and instrumentalise non-human forms of the counterpart (such as plants, animals and, yes, machines). For these reasons the challenges of our time provide good reasons for thinking about whether we should develop an alternative, non-humanistic view of people and the world that would suggest a corresponding alternative way of attributing responsibility.[10]

Forty years ago Hannah Arendt pointed out the fundamental tie of human being to an imagined counterpart. People, Arendt argues, are never completely alone, even in their thoughts; each of us conducts an inner dialogue with ourself. Every relationship a person engages in is an expression of this. Outwardly this fact is shown in the fact that human beings can only act and speak communally. Just like inner thought, outward action always requires a counterpart. According to Arendt, human beings cannot even act in the strict sense without other human beings.[11]

From this approach it is only a short step to seriously process-based and relational definitions of autonomy, personal identity, capacity to act and responsibility, such as can be found in critical post-humanist thinkers such as Donna Haraway, Rosie Braidotti and Karen Barad. Here responsibility is no longer an ability, competence or characteristic that can be attributed to or denied of a single human creature, but responsibility first develops in the interplay between several human and non-human othernesses. Donna Haraway thus does not sound completely unlike Arendt when she says that relation is the smallest unit of ontological analysis.[12] And for Rosi Bradotti, too, identity is not static and fixed, but relational and dynamic – and so are the competences that go with it: 'Identity for me is a play of multiple, fractured aspects of the self; it is relational, in that it requires a bond to the 'other'.'[13] In the end, Karen Barad argues, the individual who acts has responsibility by virtue of the structure of his or her personality, but this is always inherently shared with a counterpart or is a bond with a counterpart. Individuals do not consciously and actively decide to assume responsibility, but simply cannot do other than be responsible.[14] In Barad's thought there is an overlap between the concept of a relational ontology, in which there are no objects, entities or correlates independent of each other, and the idea of a concept of responsibility that contains an ontology that is always political, so that responsibility is always understood as in a strong sense relational. Inevitably similar approaches can be found in classical studies of responsibility that involve similarly strong attributions of individual responsibility, for example (in addition to Hannah Arendt) in Hans Jonas' *The Imperative of Responsibility* (1984), Iris Marion Young's *Responsibility for Justice* (2011) and Emmanuel Levinas' 'The Trace of the Other' (1963).

Whether this approach enables us to meet all the challenges we encounter in situations in which the traditional concept of responsibility seems to reach its limits, must here remain open. Nonetheless Barad, Braidotti and Haraway firmly suggest a serious transformation of responsibility (and other classic humanistic attributes of human existence). It is now for us to decide whether we are serious about the hype about strong concepts mentioned at the beginning of this article and radically transform responsibility, or prefer to work with more moderate gradations of the traditional understanding of responsibility such as the example of the responsibility network I described.

Translated by Francis McDonagh

Notes

1. See Luciano Floridi, *The Fourth Revolution. How the Infosphere is Reshaping Human Reality*, Oxford 2014.
2. See Janina Loh, *Trans-und Posthumanismus zur Einführung*, Hamburg, 2018.
3. 'Responsibility' and 'responsible' in English are derived from 'response', meaning 'answer'. Hence the phrase 'to answer for' and the synonym 'answerable' ('for' and 'to'). See, e.g. Merriam-Webster Online: https://www.merriam-webster.com/dictionary/responsibility. See Kurt Bayertz, 'Eine kurze Geschichte der Herkunft der Verantwortung', Kurt Bayertz (ed.), *Verantwortung. Prinzip oder Problem?* Darmstadt, 1995, pp 3–71; Hans Lenk, and Matthias Maring, article 'Verantwortung', in Joachim Ritter (ed.), *Historisches Wörterbuch der Philosophie*. Vol.11, Basle, 2007, pp 566–575.
4. For more detail on this, see Janina Sombetzki (now Loh), *Verantwortung als Begriff, Fähigkeit, Aufgabe. Eine Drei-Ebenen-Analyse*, Wiesbaden, 2014; Janina Loh (née Sombetzki), 'Strukturen und Relata der Verantwortung', Ludger Heidbrink, Claus Langbehn, and Janina Loh (ed.), *Handbuch Verantwortung*, Wiesbaden, 2017, pp 35–56.
5. Both terms in quotation marks are taken from Hans Lenk and Matthias Maring, article 'Verantwortung', in Joachim Ritter (ed.), *Historisches Wörterbuch der Philosophie*. Vol.11, Basle, 2007, p. 72.
6. Both quotations come from Hans Lenk and Matthias Maring, 'Wer soll Verantwortung tragen? Probleme der Verantwortungsverteilung in komplexen (soziotechnischen-sozioökonomischen) Systemen', Kurt Bayertz (ed.), Verantwortung. Prinzip oder Problem?, Darmstadt, 1995, p. 250. This and the following attribution models were adopted by Lenk and Maring from Richard T. DeGeorge, *Business Ethics*, New York, 1986, pp 98-9==9.
7. On responsibility for the climate, see *Sombetzki, Verantwortung als Begriff, Fähigkeit, Aufgabe. Eine Drei-Ebenen-Analyse*, pp 221-256; on responsibility in global financial markets, see Mark Coeckelbergh, *Money Machines. Electronic Financial Technologies, Distancing, and Responsibility in Global Finance*, Farnham, 2015; on responsibility in relation to autonomous driver assistance systems, see Janina Loh and Wulf Loh, 'Autonomy and responsibility in hybrid systems – the example of autonomous cars', Patrick Lin, Keith Abney, and Ryan Jenkins (ed.), *Robot Ethics 2.0. From Autonomous Cars to Artificial Intelligence*, Oxford, 2017, pp 35–50.
8. See Christian Neuhäuser, 'Roboter und moralische Verantwortung', Eric Hilgendorf (ed.), *Robotik im Kontext von Recht und Moral*, Baden-Baden, 2014, pp 269–286. I have already explained my idea of responsibility networks elsewhere; see now Janina Loh (née Sombetzki), *Verantwortung und Roboterethik – ein kleiner Überblick. Teil 2, Zeitschrift zum Innovations- und Technikrecht* (InTeR), 1/2018, 29–35.
9. An earlier version of these ideas was presented in a joint paper by Janina Loh and Mark Coeckelbergh, 'Transformation of Responsibility in the Age of Automation', Birgit Beck and Michael Köhler (ed.), *Technology, Anthropology, and Dimensions of Responsibility*, Stuttgart, 2019 (forthcoming).
10. That is a brief summary of the project of critical post-humanism, which I describe in detail in my *Einführung in den Trans- und Posthumanismus*, Hamburg, 2018.
11. See Hannah Arendt, *The Life of the Mind*, New York NY, 1978.
12. Cf Donna Haraway, *The Companion Species Manifesto: Dogs, People, and Significant Otherness*, Chicago IL, 2003.
13. Rosi Braidotti, *Nomadic Subjects. Embodiment and Sexual Difference in Contemporary Feminist Theory*, New York NY, 1994.
14. See Karen Barad, *Verschränkungen*, Berlin, 2015.

Toxic Creativity, Deep Time, and Moral Pleasure: An Ecospirituality of Technology

JACOB ERICKSON

Christian ecological theology is usually suspicious of technological creativity. With the unwieldy anthropocentric history of progress and human dominion over the ecological world, human technological creativity often is complicit in ecological waste and colonization. In our present moment, situated in the Anthropocene, how might we re-imagine human technological development in a way that re-focuses technology in the flows of planetary life? Focusing on recent 'geologic' turns in scholarship from the emergent fields of new media studies and environmental humanities, this paper argues for a new ecospirituality of technology. A 'slow' spirituality and ethic of technology might help 1) meditate on modes of disembodied, toxic creativity that contributes to ongoing forms of ecocide and ecological colonization, 2) situate moral imagination of technological progress in the 'deep time' of the planet, and 3) pay attention to the fullness of environmental despair and collaborative moral pleasure needed in the present moment.

Technology connects our planetary life together in haunting ways. Scattered around our orbit, at this very moment, shells of satellites and debris abandoned by various space programs cling to planet earth like a hazy cloud.[1] Fiber optic cables make possible near instantaneous global and virtual interconnection, all the while wrapping themselves around the

104

body of the earth in routes first carved out as the transatlantic slave trade and colonial violence. As Jenna Tiitsman notes, 'Cyberspace explicitly promises a disembodied global village as the apex of Western colonial geographical expansion.'[2] This debris and cables from space to cyberspace often hide from sight even as they embody histories into the present. And, of course, we could go on listing the ghastly: energy drained by computer servers, exploited minerals that go into making your phone, and failed economic speculations of how we might 'geo-engineer' the climate out of global warming.

Even as they physically wander a planet surrounded by material technological debris, human creatures create with an air of forgetfulness. As Sean Cubitt observes in his book *Finite Media: Environmental Implications of Digital Technologies*, 'What we imagine, in short, are consumer goods that have no history: no mines, no manufacture, no freighting, and no waste.' The privileged live lightly with what he calls the 'myth of immaterial media,' and the negative effects of environmental waste hit the global poor and indigenous hardest.[3] What we need, Cubitt and others argue, is a re-imagined geological sense of 'finite media' or finite technology that properly locates contemporary technological creativity in the lively materiality of the planet and *for* the sake of justice. New materialisms, environmental humanities, and ecological theology, we can note, now try to steer us in these directions and contexts. New media studies scholar Jussi Parikka speculates, 'Geology becomes a way to investigate materiality of the technological media world. It becomes a conceptual trajectory, a creative intervention to the cultural history of the contemporary.'[4]

As a brief, creative intervention here, my hunch is that what is needed is a new ecological spirituality of technology. As ethicist Kate Ott argues, Christian theology needs to re-imagine contemporary technological age with the affective, relational feel of the sacred earth in mind. She writes, 'Theological interconnectivity is a bit more abstract, yet no less real, and calls for an aesthetic relationship to creation can be disrupted by and also enhanced by digital technologies.'[5] Various technologies behave similar to the digital in one's discernment of the call of the sacred body of the planet. What is needed in the midst of these disruptions and enhancements is an especially *slow* ecospirituality of technology.[6] What I mean by slow is not necessarily that we grind to a halt to technological production, though there may be processes we choose to halt. Instead, a slowed down attentiveness to the textures and earthly collaborations technology might make attending to the imaginative honouring of creation more possible.[7] In doing so, we might in fact begin to pay spiritual attention to the ethical flows of human creativity, the deep material time of technology, the tragic beauty of the earth, and we may also cultivate, then, an attentive moral pleasure in our technological making.

I Toxic Creativity

Ecological theology, in its multiplicity, remains suspicious of technological development in general. In one of the most common cited genealogies of the field of religion and ecology, Lynn White, Jr. famously critiqued the anthropocentrism of humanity's claims of power, dominion, and salvation in Christianity. In doing so, he called for alternative ecospiritual models to be explored – a religious kind of remedy to a religious kind of problem. Often overlooked, however, is his attention to technological development. In his 1967 'The Historical Roots of Our Ecologic Crisis,' White calls attention to the entanglement of the dangerous *ecologic* that disregards earthly life and 'modern technology, with its ruthlessness toward nature.'[8] White's argument remains an over-cited but important touchstone in the genealogies of Christian attention to the earth.[9] Asking, like he does, about how to reclaim a sense of the animate world in our ecologic redirects our technological creativity differently in planetary ways.

Indeed, a number of scholars in White's wake worry that our technological waste is unravelling the planet. Environmental activist Bill McKibben laments that, 'We're running Genesis backward, de-creating.'[10] And Lutheran theo-ethicist Cynthia Moe-Lobeda calls that backward pull 'uncreating,' an unravelling of 'life-generating capacity.'[11] McKibben and Moe-Lobeda may very well be right, but when technological work comes into play, complex effects occur. New technologies allow for more forms of intimate communication and action, and they often create new connections just as they participate in a form of violence to the earth.

Because technology *is* creative, ecotheology needs news way of framing our technological thinking. Only then might we passionately trace technology's creative transformation in, with, and as earth. Creativity is not intrinsically good; sometimes creative acts and materials exact moral ambiguity and painful transformation.[12] Sometimes creative technologies hone an art of violence. As a placeholder, these days – instead of decreation or uncreation – I propose something like a concept like 'toxic creativity.' That our technological waste is the after-effect of a form of harmful creativity that might be able to better reflect on our current complexity. Or, to use classical language, human creativity can be distorted by sin.

Ecospirituality often focuses on the values of connection in an ecological world, cultivating resilience for doing the work of justice. It might, too, practice a richly slow attentiveness to toxic creativity, ask how creative forces are being used, ask about wise use, and work spiritual life cycle analyses on the flows of technological production. Instead of the quick desire for a technological future, we need an ethic that re-imagines technological living and justice in the context of geological deep time. In practicing spiritual attentiveness to toxic creativity, one might begin to see the complicated origins, use, and ends of our technology differently.

II Deep Timefulness

Much of our technology revolves around the toxic creativity of fast and expanding capitalist production. Phones and computers last for a short period or shopping season until a new device floods the market. Newer devices, while sometimes more efficient, sometimes require new infrastructures and better or more sources of power. Older devices become obsolete quickly and this obsolescence creates massive amounts of waste. Such devices can be difficult to dispose of and their design never took into account their disposal to begin with. Many folks, uncertain what to do, simply throw these materials away. Everything from phones to coffee pods begin to populate landfills.

Like Cubitt, Parikka, and others, geologist Marcia Bjornerud argues that we begin to consider the geological material of our technology and ecological living. The very minerals elements that make up our phones have geophysical lives that can be tracked across history. The practices of mining, extraction, and chemical reaction that make these minerals and elements into contemporary technological use also bear within themselves the marks of geophysical change. Toxic creativity can level mountains, shift atmospheric conditions, make air unbreathable, unleash pesticides into ecosystems, and can exploit other human beings in various forms of environmental racism, colonialism, sexism, and heterosexism.

Bjornerud argues that people, especially shaped in North American forms of capitalism, live with a concept of 'timelessness.' Things will go on, regardless of one's actions. Media images of youth imply the desire for living forever, or that an ecosystem or geophysical feature is permanent and unchanging. One feature of toxic creativity is technological action with that precise notion of timelessness – companies aim for 'progress,' better development, and don't necessarily plan for the disposal of new technologies even as they plan to make old technologies obsolete.

Theologically, we might see the dangerous lure of timelessness in the ways that Christianity speaks about eschatology. Life after death, redemption narratives, and a tendency towards disembodied spirit all shape everyday patterns of timelessness that disregard of the finite materiality of our planet. Dominion is imagined as a timeless human right given by a timeless Divinity.

Rather than timelessness, however, Bjornerud suggests 'timefulness' (a word that might evoke associations with 'mindfulness' or 'mindful attention'). She argues that practices of attention to the long histories of the geophysical world matter. Setting our ecological thought in the context of and in collaboration with that planetary time might help make our creativity more timely and full of present time. To pay attention to the long transformation of the minerals that make up products like phones and computers is to pay attention to all of the forces that bring those things into being. To pay attention to the patterns of decay and disposal of goods is to plan for their return to the earth in healthy ways. As Bjornerud helpfully states, 'In other words, it is time for all the sciences to adopt a geologic respect for time and its capacity to transfigure, destroy, renew, amplify, erode, propagate, entwine, innovate, and exterminate. Fathoming deep time is arguably geology's single greatest contribution to humanity.'[13] And those fathoms might be an important dimension to delve in ecospiritual work.[14]

Attention to geologic time dominates current environmental thought. Eugene Stoermer and Paul Crutzen popularized re-naming our current geological era as the Anthropocene – the time of pervasive human influence (and that includes technological) upon the earth.[15] Nothing remains untouched by human history or anthropogenic activity around the planet. We face, then, the sixth great mass extinction (caused by humans), ocean acidification (caused by humans), and global warming (caused by humans).

The concept of the Anthropocene instigated a multiplicity of other temporal namings: the 'Plantationocene' and the violent impact of the slave trade, the 'Pyrocene' and the burning of fossil fuels, and the 'Capitalocene' and the time of global exploitative economies.[16] Attention to earth and time is slowly exposing the entanglements of planetary change and human exploitation. In her stunning *A Billion Black Anthropocenes or None*, Kathryn Yusoff notes that geology is anything but neutral.[17] The language of the Anthropocene can make it seem like our present technological and climatological situation on the planet is uniformly caused by the human species. The extractive economies of geology also aligned themselves with extractive and violent logics of White supremacy, human slavery, and European colonialism.

Practicing a deep timefulness – attentive to flows of creativity and creation – is a spirituality rooted in solidarity with the materiality of the earth. That solidarity with the earth is also, simultaneously, solidarity with and resistant to ongoing flows of extractive colonialism. A spirituality of deep time practices a form of incarnational solidarity, revelling and celebrating a timeful finitude that Divinity delights in throughout creation. Might one re-imagine Divinity becoming flesh as an affirmation of the 'timeful' and finite ways the planet flows in life? Divinity's delight in creation is an approach of timefulness itself, affirming each creature and each day as good while empowering resistance to extractive economies.

III The Moral Pleasure of Making

The moral dimension of emotion and affect is utterly vital here. For many, the moral complexity of environmental problems overwhelms human moral agency, personal and collective. In her important piece 'Working Through Environmental Despair,' Joanna Macy observes the immense emotional strain those in tune with ecological collapse face. Practicing timefulness with our technology sets us face to face with our worst nightmares – social injustice, the uncertainty of global warming, and the loss of places we love. The losses exceed our own understanding.[18]

109

Environmental despair is a something we must, according to Macy, 'work through.' The double meaning of that phrase is important. We must work through, get through the overwhelming despair that plagues our moral imaginations. And we must use that despair to recognize the tremendous power and agency of human compassion. Macy writes that, 'We urgently need to find better ways of dealing with this fear and repression. Can we sustain our gaze upon the prospects of ecological holocaust without becoming paralyzed with fear or grief? Can we acknowledge and live with our pain for the world in ways that affirm our existence and release our power to act?'[19] Attentiveness to grief, sadness, concern, memory, or loss opens up a kind of political empathy that can be channelled into personal and collective action. Working through this pain, releases mental anguish and offers a way forward through connection.

As environmental writer Trebbe Johnson writes in her book *Radical Joy for Hard Times: Finding Meaning and Making Beauty in Earth's Broken Places*, 'until we allow ourselves to grieve, we will keep shutting ourselves off from the emotional bond we have with the living world and try to persuade ourselves that our concern is purely rational. And if it's reason that stauches our tears, reason can also prevent us from doing something bold, wild, and passionate to express our love.'[20] Reason will tell individuals that ecological loss is 'too big' a problem to meaningfully address. A wild and bold attentiveness, a care for the 'lives' and 'uses' of technological objects urge creative and expansive shifts of moral imagination with a lighter touch on the earth. The argument, reasonable so, that causes everyday moral agents to convince themselves nothing can be meaningfully needs emotional intelligence, grief, and the moral daring of loving action.

Finally, however, grief is not enough for our making. Environmentalists are often accused of being too serious or morose. Ecological despair often sucks the pleasure of moral creative work out of the room. But, as Nicole Seymour argues, sometimes we need to sit with, in our moment, 'the absurdities and ironies, often *through* absurdity and irony, as well as related affects and sensibilities such as irreverence, ambivalence, camp, frivolity, indecorum, awkwardness, sardonicism, perversity, playfulness, and glee.'[21] Pleasure must be re-framed in a moral fashion to lure us to new ways of enjoying the deep time of technological objects and their afterlives. We need to cultivate resilience by learning to laugh at ourselves from time to time, feeling through the pleasure of creativity when acts of care and acts of justice result.

Environmental activist and writer Naomi Klein writes in her book *No is Not Enough* that folks concerned about earth, including those engaged in religious traditions, need to engage in a more holistic program. She notes, 'What we need are *integrated* solutions, concrete ideas for how to radically bring down emissions while creating huge numbers of unionized jobs and delivering meaningful justice to those who have been abused and excluded under the current extractive economy.'[22] Integrated solutions in the hazy cloud of our moment require the whole of our making, the moral pleasure of our making, the moral emotions of what we create and what we love. We must immerse our lives in the timefulness of a vibrantly creative divinity and a vibrantly creative earth.

Notes

1. This space trash served as the inspiration for the fictions of Alfonso Cuarón's 2013 film, *Gravity*, whereby orbiting space debris sets off a chain reaction imperilling astronauts and a cascade effect that destroys various satellites and space stations. The image of a 'littered' Earth surrounded by a debris field can also be seen in the final shot of Disney's 2008 film *WALL-E*, where Earth is rendered inhabitable by various hinted-at human made catastrophe and dirt hangs around the planet like a cloud. In real life, NASA's Orbital Debris Program Office tracks tens of thousands of larger pieces of debris and hundreds of thousands of pieces of 'space junk' of all kinds.

2. Jenna Tiitsman,'Planetary Subjects after the Death of Geography' in *Planetary Loves: Spivak, Postcoloniality, and Theology*. Eds, Stephen D Moore and Mayra Rivera. New York: Fordham University Press, 2011: 162.

3. Sean Cubitt, *Finite Media: Environmental Implications of Digital Technologies*. Durham, NC: Duke University Press, 2017: 13-14.

4. He continues, 'The stories we tell imply more than just their words; they tell stories of media and mediation, of materiality and the earth.' See: Jussi Parikka, *A Geology of Media*. Minneapolis, MN: University of Minnesota Press, 2015: pages 4 and 20, respectively.

5. Chapter 4 DRAFT, pre-copy edit, used with the author's permission. Kate Ott, *Christian Ethics for a Digital Society*. Lanham, MD: Rowman & Littlefield, 2019.

6. I'm in deep sympathy with Marvin M. Ellison's approach to his book on sexual ethics here: 'Just as the slow food movement offers a creative alternative to fast food consumption, this book is a project in slow-down ethics, asking us to sit with perplexing, even discomforting questions, listen to fresh and sometimes challenging perspectives, and patiently work out matters the best we can.' See *Making Love Just: Sexual Ethics for Perplexing Times*. Minneapolis, MN: Fortress Press, 2012: 3.

7. I've written about such collaborations elsewhere as 'theophanic attunement' or 'epiphanic attentiveness' in my current writing. See my 'Theophanic Materiality: Political Ecology, Inhuman Touch, and the Art of Andy Goldsworthy' in *Entangled Worlds: Religion, Science, and New Materialisms*. Eds. Catherine Keller and Mary-Jane Rubenstein. New York: Fordham University Press, 2017: 203-220.

8. Lynn White, Jr. 'The Historical Roots of Our Ecologic Crisis.' *Science*, New Series, Vol. 155, No. 3767. (Mar. 10, 1967): 1205.

9. See Matthew Riley's important work in reclaiming a larger sense of White's sense of technology and democracy. See Riley's essay 'A Spiritual Democracy of All God's Creatures: Ecotheology and the Animals of Lynn White, Jr.' in *Divinanimality: Animal Theory, Creaturely Theology*. Ed. Stephen Moore. New York: Fordham University Press, 2014. See also Willis Jenkins' essay, 'After Lynn White: Religious Ethics and Environmental Problems' *Journal of Religious Ethics*. June 2009.

10. Bill McKibben, *Eaarth: Making a Life on a Tough New Planet*. New York: Times Books, 2010: 25.

11. Cynthia Moe-Lobeda, *Resisting Structural Evil: Love as an E4cological-Economic Vocation*. Minneapolis, MN: Fortress Press, 2013: 56.

12. Of course, on this feature of creativity, see Catherine Keller's *Face of the Deep: A Theology of Becoming*. New York: Routledge, 2003.

13. Marcia Bjornerud. *Timefulness: How Thinking Like a Geologist Can Help Save the World*. Princeton, NJ: Princeton University Press, 2018: 16.

14. Indeed, it already is in many thinkers from Joseph Sittler's theology of the earth to Ivone Gebara's multiplicity in creation to Thomas Berry's universe story.

15. Andrew C. Revkin recounts part of this history in 'Confronting the 'Anthropocene'' *The New York Times*. Online: http://dotearth.blogs.nytimes.com/2011/05/11/confronting-the-anthropocene/ Published May 11th, 2011.

16. See, for example, Donna J. Haraway's important recent work, *Staying with the Trouble: Making Kin in the Chthulucene*. Minneapolis, MN: University of Minnesota Press, 2016. And Steven J. Pyne's writing on 'The Fire Age' *Aeon Magazine*. Online: http://aeon.co/magazine/science/how-our-pact-with-fire-made-us-what-we-are/

17. Kathryn Yusoff. *A Billion Black Anthropocenes or None*. Minneapolis, MN: University of Minnesota Press, 2018.

18. The Australian philosopher Glenn Albrecht called this feeling 'solastalgia,' for the pain of a loss of a comforting place. It's a neologism of the Latin 'solacium,' which means 'comfort,' and the Greek 'algia,' which means 'pain.' See his 'Ecoparalysis,' Healthearth blog, January 31, 2010. Web: http://healthearth.blogspot.com/2010/01/ecoparalysis.html

19. Joanna Macy, 'Working Through Environmental Despair,' *Ecosychology*, Roszak, Gomes, & Kanner, eds., Sierra Club 1995: 10.

20. Trebbe Johnson, *Radical Joy for Hard Times: Finding Meaning and Making Beauty in Earth's Broken Places*. Berkeley, CA: North Atlantic Books, 2018: 48.

21. Nicole Seymour, Bad Environmentalism: Irony and Irreverence in the Ecological Age. Minneapolis, MN: University of Minnesota Press, 2018: 4.

22. Naomi Klein, *No is Not Enough*. New York: Penguin Books, 2017: 238.

Part Four: Theological Forum

Instances of Theological Renewal Starting Out From the Council

ENRICO GALAVOTTI

The half-century which separates us from the conclusion of the Second Vatican Council represents sufficient time to ascertain to what extent the conciliar event had a fundamental impact on the re-definition of the status and tasks of theology. The Council came about at a time that was also full of impetus aimed at renewing theological work, which had also been subject to a systematic campaign of devitalisation. Re-reading today the interventions of the Roman magisterium from the last half century which preceded the announcement of John XXIII's decision to convoke the Second Vatican Council, one is struck by frequently recurring phrases which became the very object of suspicion and censure: 'new' and 'newness' were read as synonymous with heterodoxy, deviation from correct faith, and the assumption of criteria of discernment other than those traditionally indicated by the Roman magisterium, with all the consequences for supporters of such novelty. We know that this was also the attitude which guided the drafting of the preparatory schema for Vatican II, in which the best minds of the Roman theological school produced treatises which intended to safe-guard the Christian faith, considered to be constantly threatened by an enemy who, from time to time, from decade to decade, assumed this or that face.[1] The inaugural speech of the Council given by John XXIII cleared the field of many misunderstandings: the Pope made it clear that Vatican II had not been called to sanction new condemnations, but to determine the Church's 'aggiornamento':[2] it was increasingly necessary in a world where, as Yves Congar had written a year previously, 'one person in four is Chinese; one in three lives under a Communist regime: one Christian in every two is a non-Catholic'.[3] Shortly before the start of Vatican II, John XXIII had in fact confided that whoever had drawn up the preparatory schema had not understood that the Council could not nor should be a theological congress, and even less a congress against someone or something.[4]

In effect, the Council which ended in 1965 with the outcomes which we all know also represented a radical change in theology both as regards method and its main interests. This fact can be evaluated empirically simply by comparing the manuals in use in theology faculties before and after Vatican II. Before the Council, these manuals, even if written by different authors, constantly presented the same structure and the same content. The dogmatic manuals of Tanquerey or of Billot formed decades of generations up to the threshold of Vatican II. In the well-known *Enciclopedia Cattolica* Cardinal Parente wrote that in Billot's manual 'the most arduous questions find a solution which can be believed to be definitive'.[5] The preparation of these texts was perfectly expressive of the way of thinking and working for the majority of theologians of that era: the main concern was to stay within the lines already traced by authoritative predecessors, limiting oneself to minimal adjustments. And precisely in commenting on this way of the theologians' working, Carl Jung observed: '[theological thinkers] are so used to dealing with eternal truths that they know no other kinds. When the physicist says that the atom is of such and such a composition, and when he sketches a model of it, he too does not intend to express anything like an eternal truth. But theologians do not understand the natural sciences, and, particularly, psychological thinking'.[6] As is well known, it was a theology with a deductive system, which had developed a concept of tradition which, in reality, was much more confined chronologically than its proponents were aware, dating back at most to the interpretation given by the Council of Trent. Assuming this approach, even the Bible was downgraded as source of Revelation and was reduced to a legislative codex designed to confirm the compositions of theologians. It was a situation nourished also by the centralising tendency of the Roman papacy following on from the First Vatican Council, which ensured that every papal pronouncement, leaving aside its specific object, even if it did not make explicit recourse to infallibility, assumed definitive value.[7] Theology produced by the Roman school, which exercised a dominant role within this process, therefore had a heavy responsibility with regard to the impoverishment of the very function of theology.[8]

The Second Vatican Council put an end to this deviation and opened new perspectives: and those manuals which until a few years earlier had been described as definitive now suddenly appeared to be useless and out of context. It was the effect of the change in the status of theology determined by the Council: because Vatican II, tackling crucial questions such as the liturgical dimension, the sources of Revelation, the relationship with the modern world, and dialogue with other religions, committed theologians to a profound renewal of reflection and their own methods of re-search, drastically re-shaping recourse to the deductive method. They were all questions which in part were well known to theology, but which now needed to be understood by theology in a different way than in the past. In fact the Council Fathers had to acknowledge how the major scientific progress of the last decades had shaped, not just a world very different from that in which the previous Council had been celebrated, but above all a different way of thinking in everyone. The Pastoral Constitution on the Church in the Modern World spoke in this way about the 'scientific mentality' which 'has brought about a change in the cultural sphere and on habits on thought, and the progress of technology is now reshaping the face of the earth and has its sights set on the conquest of space [...]. The accelerated pace of history is such that one can scarcely keep abreast of it. The destiny of the human race is viewed as a complete whole, no longer, as it were, in the particular histories of various peoples: now it merges into a complete whole. And so humankind substitutes a dynamic and more evolutionary concept of nature for a static one, and the result is an immense series of new problems calling for a new endeavour of analysis and synthesis' (*Gaudium et spes*, n. 5). Here as in so many other passages of the conciliar *corpus*, the bishops thus let it be understood that precisely the awareness of being integrated in dynamics which were extraordinarily new and far from being concluded, allowed them to launch processes of reform and re-thinking: they no longer presumed, as their predecessors had, to resolve them again with ironclad formula.[9] And in fact, when Vatican II sought to go into too much detail, as in the Decree on the Means of Social Communications *Inter mirifica*, it ended up by producing texts which were already out of date at the point of their final approval.

Ultimately, the Fathers of Vatican II posited a new way of approaching the heart of Christian Revelation, with the knowledge that even the ancient Scripture-Tradition duality could no longer contain its totality. It was also to salvation history, that is, the history of humanity, that we would have to turn to from now on to grasp the fullness of Christian Revelation. While in fact pre-conciliar theology imagined Revelation as the way in which God communicated his own teachings to men and women, the Council Fathers had already reached the conclusion that it 'unfolds through deeds and words which are intrinsically connected: the works performed by God in the history of salvation show forth and confirm the doctrine and realities signified by the words; the words, for their part, proclaim the works, and bring to light the mystery they contain. The most intimate truth thus revealed about God and human salvation shines forth for us in Christ, who is himself both the mediator and the sum total of revelation' (*Dei verbum*, n. 2).[10] So Vatican II offered a different perspective for the understanding of Revelation, showing how, precisely because it interfaces constantly with the history of humanity, is constantly susceptible to in-depth analysis. Historical events be-come clearer in their implications the more we can observe them from a more distant perspective; and our present, too, which we often imagine being able to understand in all its implications – even more so in an era where we are immersed in a constant and immense flow of data and information – is in reality susceptible to a re-reading and to a re-understanding which to us today is not possible. In the same way, beginning with the Council, it has become ever clearer that Revelation has a density of content which was unknown both to those who were the direct protagonists of the events narrated in Scripture, and to those who concretely participated in the redactional process of the biblical text.

Thus the Council committed theologians to seeking to undertake the effort of a new understanding of the Word of God, to investigating precisely that plurality of meanings which still waits to be highlighted. In the Bull convoking the Council (1961) and in the Encyclical *Pacem in terris* (1963), Pope John had again taken up the gospel image of the 'signs of the times', trying to understand where they might be recognisable in the society of his time. It was and is a huge task, because such 'signs' are never identifiable in what is more obvious, pleasant, reassuring or solemn, but always recognisable in humility, in the hidden, in what happens without arousing turmoil. And if we re-read the conciliar texts assuming this theological perspective we easily become aware of how the Fathers were able to acknowledge that their task, at that precise historical moment, was not to reach conclusive points, as those who had prepared the preparatory steps for the council which Pius XII in the end decided not to convoke had imagined, but rather to make all Christians understand that they were within a salvation history in a continuous state of becoming and which therefore demanded a spirit of permanent research.

It is essential, therefore, that a task of a cultural nature is assigned to theology starting from the Second Vatican Council. A well-known Italian director recalled shortly before his death that culture must not be confused with notionism or erudition: it is possible to be a people of culture even with little or no education, because culture is the total awareness of the space in which one lives, of the profound processes and the boundaries which characterise the world in which one lives. In the last half century, therefore, theology has been assigned an even more important task than the one under-taken in past centuries, precisely because it has been committed to investigating every aspect of human life in order to grasp its meaning in the light of Christian Revelation. Starting from the Council, theology has had to renounce its own certainty, as well as the idea of its own primacy over other sciences. It is a process which had certainly begun well before Vatican II: suffice to think of the status of theology at the time when the great universities arose.[11] The shock of the revolution of the Enlightenment seemed to have permanently marked the fate of theological reflection, and yet, precisely when theology seemed to be heading towards its own extinction, it suddenly regained centrality: not in the sense of a recovery of positions of dominance, but rather through the entrusting of a role in finding answers about the meaning and role of Christians in an ever-developing world.[12] This is significant and means continually immersing oneself in Christian communities: to understand their difficulties and contradictions, and to seek to identify a way to be able to make the gospel of Jesus of Nazareth resonate once again.[13] But it also means acknowledging that not all the answers can be found in Scripture, as happened at the Council of Nicaea, when to compose the

Creed the Fathers had recourse to a term, *homousios*, which was not contained within the biblical canon. Theology thus showed itself to be more pluralist and sensitive to the cultural profiles of the Christian people and, even though with reticence and resistance, also set aside the ancient tendency to list errors and impose condemnations, which was determined precisely by the conviction that it was the world which had to fit to what the magisterium prescribed.

So we are faced with a new theology, both in terms of working methods and the objectives on which it sets it sights. This is significant also for acknowledging the insufficiency of Vatican II: in the sense that precisely in how it was imposed, the Council anticipated the start of a journey (the start of a beginning, Rahner described it) which still remains largely to be completed. Here, too, I will limit myself to a comment: in the last twenty years there has been no shortage of historians, some authoritative, too, who believe that the reception of Vatican II was represented by the pontificate of John Paul II. In the light of what happened and is happening starting from the election of Pope Francis (one thinks of the ecumenical gestures, the re-modelling of the functioning of the Synod of Bishops, the stimuli given to collegiality and to synodality, the criteria now followed for episcopal appointments and the creation of cardinals) can this statement still be considered to be appropriate? Or rather is the current pontificate, even unwittingly, becoming precisely the litmus test for what had never been done for the purposes of the reception of the Council? Of course, the awareness of being in the midst of a ford generates distress, even in theologians. In this sense I believe it is exemplary that the debate that has arisen around the reception of the Exhortation *Amoris Laetitia*, which beyond the concrete solutions proposed prescribes above all the assumption of new criteria of discernment, which are the consequence of the theologians' different way of working in the current circumstance. Starting from Vatican II, theology therefore has had to acknowledge the failure of a certain biblical positivism, as well as of the rigid formulation legal prêt-à-porter theology expressed by Denzinger.[14]

Today the Church recognises it is no longer in possession of all the tools to fulfil its own evangelising mission and this, too, is the reason why, in the post-conciliar period, it has often been seen that the documents produced by individual bishops or bishops gathered at the regional level are pre-ceded by a series of sociological analyses. The Church has finally understood that it is in the history of humanity that it is possible to gather data still not understood about the Christian truth: after all, already Gregory the Great, a pope called to lead the Church at a time of profound crisis, where there was the widespread conviction about the imminent extinction of Christianity, recalled that 'the sacred Scriptures grow with the one who reads them'.[15] Theology sprung from Vatican II has thus made its own the invitation of John XXIII on his death bed: 'Today more than ever, certainly more than in past centuries, we are called to serve mankind as such, and not merely Catholics; to de-fend above all and everywhere the rights of the human person and not merely those of the Catholic Church. Today's world, the needs made plain in the last fifty years and a deeper understanding of doctrine have brought us to a new situation, as I said in the address at the opening of the Council. It is not that the Gospel has changed: it is that we have begun to understand it better'.[16]

Translated by Patricia Kelly

Notes

1. A. Indelicato, *Difendere la dottrina o annunciare l'Evangelo. Il dibattito nella Commissione centrale preparatoria del Vaticano II*, Genoa 1992.
2. Cfr. G. Alberigo, *Formazione, contenuto e fortuna dell'allocuzione, in Fede tradizione profezia. Studi su Giovanni XXIII e sul Vaticano II*, Brescia 1984, pp. 187-222.
3. Y. Congar, *My Journal of the Council*, Liturgical Press 2012, p. 41.
4. G. Sale, *Giovanni XXIII e la preparazione del Concilio Vaticano II nei diari inediti del direttore della 'Civiltà Cattolica' padre Roberto Tucci*, Jaca Book, Milan 2012, p. 150.
5. C. Molari, *La teologia incontra la vita, in 'Jesus'*, XV (1993), 3, p. 53.
6. Cited in ibidem.
7. Cfr. A. Melloni, *Definitivus/definitive*, in 'Cristianesimo nella Storia', XXI (2000), 1, pp. 171-205, and J.-F. CHIRON, *L'infaillibilité et son objet. L'autorité du magistère infaillible de l'Église s'étend-elle aux vérités non révélées?*, Paris 1999.
8. S. Adamiak-s. Tanzarella, *La teologia romana dei secoli XIX e XX, in Costantino I. Enciclopedia costantiniana sulla figura e l'immagine dell'imperatore del cosiddetto Editto di Milano, 313-2013*, Rome 2013, pp. 377-389.
9. On the linguistic development undertaken by Vatican II, see J. O'Malley, *What happened at Vatican II*, First Harvard University Press 2010.
10. On the laborious redactional process behind this Constitution see R. Burigana, *La Bibbia nel Concilio. La redazione della costituzione 'Dei Verbum' del Vaticano II*, Il

Mulino, Bologna 1998

11. M.D. Chenu, *La teologia nel XII secolo*, Milan 1986.

12. Cfr. *Dizionario teologico*, eds. J.B. Bauer and C. Molari, Assisi 1974, pp. 12-15.

13. Cfr. G. Ruggieri, *Cristianesimo, chiese e vangelo*, Bologna 2002.

14. J. Schumacher, *Der Denzinger. Geschichte und Bedeutung eines Buches in der Praxis der neueren Theologie*, Freiburg 1974; in his writings Rahner often alluded to the risks of 'Denzinger-Theologie'.

15. Cfr. P.C. Bori, *L'interpretazione infinita. L'ermeneutica cristiana antica e le sue trasformazioni*, Bologna 1987.

16. L. Capovilla, *Giovanni XXIII. Quindici letture*, Rome 1970, p. 475.

Theology in Italy Today

LEONARDO PARIS

In this contribution I seek to offer a sketch of theology in Italy.[1] I do not purport to identify a style or characteristics of Italian theology as such – they probably do not exist – but rather to identify certain aspects of the context, some opportunities and risks, and finally, some possible changes which face theology in Italy today. In so doing I will endeavour to bear in mind the Foreword to the Apostolic Constitution *Veritatis Gaudium* (VG)[2] in the conviction that in that systematic text some of the most significant hopes for the theology of today and tomorrow are expressed.

I Context

The context of theology in Italy has several quite specific characteristics, which derive from a series of very precise relationships.

The first relationship is that between the academic institutions of theology.

There are three, different, types of institutions involved.[3]

(1) There are 8 Facoltà Teologiche Italiane (Italian Faculties of Theology), in Milan, Padua, Bologna, Florence, Naples, Palermo, Bari, and Cagliari, with 5 parallel departments. This number excludes the 12 Roman Theology Faculties, and the Waldensian Faculty of Theology, which are not strictly speaking Italian, but Vatican and/or international, either from a juridical perspective or from the perspective of the audience for which they are designed.

(2) The 47 or so Istituti Teologici Affiliati, Aggregati e Incorporati (Affiliated, Aggregated and Incorporated Theological Institutes). These exist mainly to form clergy, and there are large differences among them

in quality and numbers. This reflects a choice – that of maintaining diocesan seminaries, with often reduced numbers but strong local links, or of creating larger inter-diocesan seminaries – which has given rise to different kinds of seminaries in Italy.

(3) Finally, the Istituti Superiori di Scienze Religiose (Higher Institutes of Religious Studies). These are predominantly concerned with the formation of teachers of Catholic religious studies, but are also attended by those lay people who are interested in theology. They were recently involved in an upgrading process which saw their numbers reduced by almost half to 48. The uncertainty of the status of religious studies means that while the course of studies at various points looks very similar to that at the universities and the seminaries, the major difference is that the ISSR do not give a first degree, and therefore cannot allow students to progress to Masters and Doctoral studies.

From this we have two consequences: a certain separation of the paths taken by clergy and laity, and a certain scattering, overlap, and confusion in courses of studies.

The second relationship is with the state universities.

Neither theological studies nor religious studies are incorporated into the offerings at state universities. This is for deep historical reasons and is evidence of the mutual suspicion between Church and State, whose analysis is beyond the scope of this article.

The effect of this separation is a certain isolation of theology both with respect to other disciplines and more generally with respect to the national intellectual debate. Often the theologians who find a space in the television, journalistic, and academic cultures in Italy are not those who are part of the academic theological institutions.

The third relationship is between Italian theology and the world of the Magisterium and the pontifical universities.

The fact that Italy has such close links with the Vatican brings with it a balance of relationships which are difficult to manage, and which offer obvious advantages and disadvantages. A major relevant aspect is the presence in Italy of another level of theological institutions – the Roman universities – which are not in fact Italian in either the provenance of their faculty members, nor in their frames of reference.

One of the advantages is certainly the fact that the many theologians throughout the world who have often pursued their Licence or Doctoral studies in Rome know Italian. One of the disadvantages is the fact that the close presences of these central Vatican bodies risks giving Italian theology a certain sense of permanent 'compulsory administration'. Paradoxically there is also a risk of not encouraging international comparisons, given the illusion of already having internationalisation 'at home'.

II Characteristics
There are three characteristics which mark Italian theology compared to other European and international theological contexts.

The first characteristic is a very solid ecclesial link. Italian theology operates in a context in which Christianity is still alive and practised, even if with great differences. The theologian does speak first of all to other theologians, but to living ecclesial reality. The call addressed by the Pope to the Italian Theological Association 'practise theology in the Church'[4] is a snapshot of what is already happening and invitation to continue along this path rather than a suggestion to change tack. It remains common that the professional theologian is either a priest, or a lay person who also undertakes significant pastoral work.

The second characteristic is an undefined cultural link. It cannot be said that Italian culture is hostile or indifferent to Christian themes, and yet it is as if dialogue was barely present or incisive. It is as if the theologians in the Italian cultural context did not listen and were not heard. Here one sees perhaps the fruit of a confrontation with the culture of the Enlightenment and the scientific revolution which never completely happened; it is a problem which can be seen in a lot of theology, not just Italian. However, in Italy this has a great impact and is clearly a challenge to Italian theology.

The third characteristic is the level of theological production. It seems to me that not only is Italian theological output very good, but it is also very widespread. Numerous theological associations contribute in a decisive manner to this dissemination, the most important of which have been gathered together for twenty years in the *Co-ordination of the Italian Theological Associations* (CATI). The significant fact is that such output is not often recognised neither at international or national level, sometimes not even by those responsible for it. As in many others areas, Italians seem inclined to be the first to not recognise their own value and to uncritically overrate what comes from elsewhere.

At this point some fundamental challenges can be identified, challenges which, in my opinion, constitute the tasks which Italian theology could take on to be faithful to its own history and to the time we are living.

III Italian theology for Italy

Over the next few years Italy as a whole will be facing changes which cannot be forecast in detail, but which will probably result in a society much more pluralist, multi-cultural and multi-religious that the majority of Italians desire. Theology will probably not be able to change this nor provide everyone with the resources to understand and experience this change.

But its role should be to establish a more significant cultural dialogue with Italian society overall, learning to be *one voice* within society itself. That means providing it with hermeneutical, theological, and descriptive tools which can also speak to non-religious or different religious public contexts, succeeding in expressing its own *voice* to establish a fruitful dialogue. That also means learning to be only one of the voices which determine the social space.[6]

This is especially evident in the political arena. Italian Catholics are faced with models which can barely be deemed to be guides for the future: both the *non expedit* model,[7] which characterised Italian Catholicism from 1874 to 1919, and the model of the one party for Catholics – whose most significant example is the Democrazia Cristiana which united the majority of the Catholic electorate in the post-war period up to 1994 – expressed the idea that the Catholic one should be the only voice, or no voice. What might happen in the future depends on many factors; however, I believe theology has a completely specific role indicating the theoretical foundations and concrete style with which one can speak being simply and decisively *one voice*.

In concrete terms, one of the most difficult tasks will be that of finding the way to be able to speak about the Lord Jesus in the public sphere. Due to the strong ecclesial embedding, the risk is that discourse about Jesus, even when it is undertaken by professional theologians, assumes markedly catechetical tones. But catechesis, in principle, is addressed to Christians. The only alternative seems to be that of speaking about Jesus simply in systematic terms as an historical-social event of the past. Instead, a style which enables the integration of the Lord Jesus – with the claims, the proposals, the salvation which he brings to everyone – into everyone's space. It is precisely this style which could make fruitful for the Italian (and European) Pope Francis' invitation underlined by the first of the criteria expressed in *Veritatis Gaudium*, that of a 'joyful and life-giving contemplation of the face of God revealed in Jesus Christ' (VG 4,a). In fact such a context demands that the richness of the *kerygma* finds ways to exit the intra-ecclesial sphere and present itself to non-believers, too, as a starting-point and fruitful provocation.

It is not an easy challenge, but I believe that the task to find *a voice which speaks of Jesus* showing its theoretical, cultural, political interest can be attractive for Italian theologians and useful to both Italian believers and non-believers alike.

IV Italian theology for the Italian Church

The intra- and extra-ecclesial links of Italian theology mean that the figure of the theologian struggles to find its own autonomy in Italy, and struggles to define itself as a specific charism. The status and positioning of theology and those who exercise it are uncertain. To define this status is an important service which theology can offer to the Italian Church, from different perspectives.

In fact, in the Church theology is neither everything nor nothing. It is a part, a specific charism, because the expertise and the gifts necessary to exercise it are specific. It is not something which can be absorbed by the charism of the magisterium or by pastoral work. Where this charism is not recognised, because it is exercised largely by pastors or because it is barely defined, the other charisms also feel the impact.

Two aspects in particular are worthy of mention. The first is that the difficulty of finding a place for theologians mirrors the difficulty in finding a place for theology, that is to say, for the intellectual and critical dimensions of the faith. This can cause great harm above all in clergy formation, which today must face up to an Italian reality where it can be common to find that the 'sheep' are more educated than the 'shepherds'. For the positioning of the theological-intellectual aspect within the totality of ecclesial life and that of the believer not to be clear is not conducive to wise pastoral activity.

The second aspect is that theology could be a special place of recognition and appreciation of male and female laity, only of course if the status of the theological charism is clarified. Otherwise, it will be perceived as undue intrusion, making this sensitive relationship even more complex. Where this status is clarified it will be possible to articulate the charisms in such a way that each person – with regard to the part that belongs to them – has their own voice equipped with specific authority. Without a pluralist perception of authority the Church appears like a monolithic pyramid where the baptismal dignity of the laity is affirmed in principle, but never manifested.

In order to be carried out, the theological charism must be conscious of its own role, without being reckless, but also without being fearful; without a sense of superiority, but also without a sense of minority. This could help the Italian theologian to be more passionate, to find a more original voice and overcome certain excesses of prudence which do not make it fruitful.

V Italian theology for Europe and for the World

I think it is possible to identify the broader task of Italian theology in the international panorama by paying attention to what is happening at the level of academic theological output. Italian theologians could take on a very interesting dual task of mediation: that of mediating between the richness of the European churches in their totality towards the new and old Churches of the world.

The first mediation – from Europe towards Italy – calls for a moving away from a certain provincialism and an opening out in a more decisive manner to dialogue with European culture. This demands not only the ability to listen, but also a certain degree of courage, recognising that Italian theology, too, has something to say and give to others – thus coming out of a certain minority feeling.

The second mediation is more complex, but also more strategic. The European Churches have a history, a richness, a role, which cannot be ignored. It is essential to recognise that other Churches have the right to discover their own path, but this does not mean that all these riches and this history can be simply set aside. The task would be that of making available this patrimony for those to whom Christianity is entrusted today. Forms of mediation which allow this passage must be found.

Here Italian theology could have a special role in the realisation of this fourth criterion of *Veritatis Gaudium*, that is "networking' between those institutions worldwide that cultivate and promote ecclesiastical studies, in order to set up suitable channels of cooperation' (VG 4,d). In fact it has at its disposal a language known by many theologians throughout the world, a propensity – which derives from contact with Vatican structures – to think taking into account the broad horizon of the world, and good systematic quality. Above all, it has an ecclesial reality sufficiently alive through which it is possible to appreciate in the flesh theological intuitions and proposals. Theological ideas and contributions can be verified 'as it were, 'on the ground' thanks to the persevering commitment to a social and cultural meditation on the Gospel undertaken by the People of God' according to a model of 'performative interpretation of the reality' (VG 3). At the same time this enables the understanding of what is arising in the European universities and from the European ecclesial experiences, including the Italian ones, and to translate it and offer it in an appropriate fashion to other ecclesial experiences throughout the world.

This is a mediation which involves the ability to think about one's own experience in linguistic, cultural, and conceptual terms which can be translated and offered also to those who live in very different experiential, linguistic, cultural, and conceptual contexts.

As an Italian theologian and Christian, I see clearly the limitations of this perspective. And yet I also see the richness which could stem from the courageous assumption of these tasks. In any case I believe it is fundamental to identify the challenges which the current circumstances place before theology, and try to tackle them: not just as individuals and not just as a group of theologians from all over the world. The first perspective is too confined – there are challenges which cannot be tackled alone – and the second risks becoming generic – the challenges of everyone are the challenges of no-one. The totality of Italian theologians could take on some specific challenges, just as specific challenges await the theologians of other nations and other contexts.

Translated by Patricia Kelly

Notes

The author wishes to state that his contribution reproduces, with some modifications, his address given in Bologna at the *European Academy of Religion* (*First Annual Conference* 5-8 March 2018). The author also wishes to express his gratitude to those who offered ideas and suggestions for the contribution (especially: Alberto Dal Maso, Serena Noceti, Giacomo Canobbio, Simona Segoloni, Stefano Zeni, Romolo Rossini).

1. For further information and extensive bibliographical references see: S. Segoloni Ruta, 'Scenario attuale delle scuole teologiche' in *CredereOggi* 38 (6/2018), 111-123; 155-161; M. MARIANI, 'Lo studio della teologia in Italia. Verso Dove?' in *Il Regno* 63 (10/2018) 305-315.
2. http://w2.vatican.va/content/francesco/it/apost_constitutions/documents/papa-francesco_costituzione-ap_20171208_veritatis-gaudium.html
3. Cf. https://teologiaissr.chiesacattolica.it/elenco-delle-discipline-ecclesiastiche-e-delle-facolta-e-degli-istituti-che-rilasciano-titoli-validi-per-lirc/. A quick glance at the different types of institutions would immediately make clear the variety of institutions and the difficulty in providing precise figures.
4. https://w2.vatican.va/content/francesco/it/speeches/2017/december/documents/papa-francesco_20171229_associazione-teologica-italiana.html.
5. Cf. http://www.teologiacati.it. For an analysis done by the associations themselves on the status of theology in Italy, see: P. Ciardella – A. Montan (eds.), *Le scienze teologiche in Italia a cinquant'anni dal Concilio Vaticano II. Storia, impostazioni metodologiche, prospettive*, Elledici, Turin 2011.
6. It seems to me that the premise of both the third criterion of *Veritatis Gaudium* – 'wide-ranging dialogue' (VG 4,b) – and the fourth – 'inter-disciplinary and cross-disciplinary approaches carried out with wisdom and creativity' – is precisely the willingness to recognise oneself as part of a dialogue in which the speaker is not simply the one who receives the truth. Rather the truth itself involves both as communicative subjects, according to Benedict XVI's indication in *Caritas in Veritate*, 4.
7. By the *non expedit* Pope Pius IX stated it was unacceptable for Catholics to participate in the elections in the then Kingdom of Italy and more generally to participate in Italian political life.

Faith Consistent Investment Guidelines

SÉAMUS P FINN OMI

I Vatican Context

Catholic Social Teaching (CST) has offered a consistent stream of teaching and reflections on the different financial systems that countries have adopted and followed over the last 150 years. They have consistently evaluated and commented on the positive and negative features of these systems and judged their impacts through the lens of human freedom and dignity and their respect for and promotion of the common good. More recently this has included an integration and evaluation of the burden that the economic activity of both the public and private actors in these systems has visited upon the planet and local and regional ecologies.

The administration and operations of the Vatican and the policies and practices that guide its economic and temporal activities have received additional scrutiny as the CST tradition has evolved and published new ethical and moral principles and expectations for both believers, catholic institutions and catholic business leaders who operate and participate in financial transactions and commercial activities. Requests for access to the guidelines and policies that the Holy See follows in the administration and management of the temporal affairs of the Vatican City State (VCS)[1] have increased especially when they interface with sovereign and regional regulators that manage and monitor regional and global financial activities and when they use intermediary financial institutions to conduct financial transactions. Guidelines and policies for managing the fixed and liquid assets of the VCS are often included in this scrutiny especially if the Holy See advocates for certain policies when participating in public forums and recommend specific policies and actions to believers and other institutions.

II Praxis of Faith Consistent Investing (FCI)

Faith based institutional investors have engaged in the praxis of aligning the management of their assets with the beliefs, values and principles of their respective traditions for decades and in some instances even longer. This praxis emerged from a deeply held sense of moral responsibility for the ownership and management of their assets in a way that was consistent with the teaching and practice of their traditions.

In recent decades, technology has facilitated speedy access to data and transparency, made it easier for owners and investors to realize this goal and to demand greater accountability from consultants and asset managers. In addition, the availability of research and analysis of past performance data and specifically the measurement of the impact of and faith or values criteria on the financial performance of a portfolio has convinced many faith-based asset owners to include this practice in the management of their portfolios.

The documents of Vatican II and subsequent Catholic Social Teaching called for greater authenticity and integrity in reflecting the example and teaching of Christ across all aspects of ecclesial administration and operations. An example of this call is found in the synodal document 'Justice in the World' which was published in 1971 and states 'While the Church is bound to give witness to justice, she recognizes that anyone who ventures to speak to people about justice must first be just in their eyes.'[2]

Many church institutions and organizations have embraced this teaching in the management of their assets and established or adopted the policies, tools and resources to realize this objective. At least three conferences of Catholic bishops have published statements and guidelines on how to realize this vision[3] The USCCB; the Germans and the French.

III Process

In 2014 the former Pontifical Council for Justice and Peace, now the Dicastery for Promoting Integral Human Development, in conjunction with the IOR initiated a process that would lead to the publication of a document on FCI that would serve as a resource for the Holy See and for Catholic institutions and organization across the world. The document seeks to acknowledge the good work that has already been accomplished by many Catholic institutions and organizations and at the same time to encourage those who have not adopted this practice to seriously consider doing so as a witness to their Catholic identity, service to the common good and care for the earth, 'our common home'.[4]

The document reviews the teaching of the scripture on the threefold relationship between Creator, Creature and Creation and the guiding principles that are laid down to govern those relationships. 'Doing righteousness and justice' (Gen. 18:19) is realized through fidelity to God and his covenant and a reverential concern for the neighbour and creation. It then reviews the tradition in the Church Fathers and the scholastics as they reflected on the nature of 'lending', 'interest' usury and the role of banking and insurance. The final section of this review examines the core principles of Catholic Social Teaching that are presented in the Compendium of Social Doctrine[5] and in addition the principle of 'integral ecology' that is prominent in *Laudato Si'*.

After providing this foundation the document goes on to present the basic frameworks and perspectives that have informed those already active in Faith Consistent and Socially Responsible Investing. First and foremost, these include the practice of 'negative screening' which identifies those sectors, companies or activities that the faith consistent investor will want to exclude from their portfolio.

More recently many are examining more closely the practice of 'positive' social impact investing whereby investors seek to deploy their assets projects and funds whose objective is to play a constructive role in promoting development and enabling social and ecological entrepreneurship.

Finally, the document provides a list of the practical steps involved in following or establishing a Faith Consistent Investing program and identifies the policies, resources, tools that can guide those institutions that are starting out on this journey. This checklist will hopefully provide a roadmap for those who have been hesitant to take up this missionary opportunity and support constructive and conversations within institutions

IV Conclusion

The praxis of FCI and Socially Responsible Investing has evolved through several stages over the past fifty years. The recognition of the influence and power of publicly listed corporations especially those with an international and now global footprint served to awaken those shareholders to a consideration of their personal and institutional responsibility as owners. As shareholders recognized that companies relied on their capital to grow their businesses and to accelerate and expand when opportunity presented itself they also became more aware of the tools that were available to fulfil their responsibilities as owners.

In the beginning a small number of shareholders chose to avoid investing in some industry sectors all together because of their beliefs or values and others chose to engage the managers of corporations that were in their portfolios about products, policies and practices that they considered morally objectionable. Over time and through experience these efforts produced different sets of social and environmental guidelines that were considered alongside the financial guidelines that investors followed in their decision making.

Research and advances in technology have rendered these activities more accessible and reliable and therefore provided the opportunity for more investors to integrate the practices into their asset management approaches. This has included reliable research that demonstrates that the impact of the integration of social and ecological considerations into the investment process has little or no impact on the financial return.

It is hoped that the preparation and publication of this document will encourage the Church, the Vatican City State and Catholic institutions and individual believers to more fully embrace this practice and see it as an opportunity for greater alignment and integration of their beliefs into the management of their assets, promotion of the common good and care for the earth 'our common home'. In addition, the embrace of this activity will be an opportunity to shine the light and teaching of the tradition into this dimension of the financial system to infuse more wholesome and ethical principles into its operations.

Notes

1. Lateran Treaty Between The Holy See and the Kingdom of Italy (February 11, 1929), http://www.vaticanstate.va/content/dam/vaticanstate/documenti/leggi-e-decreti/ Normative-Penali-e-Amministrative/LateranTreaty.pdf. For a scholarly exploration of the VCS's legal structure, see Stephen E. Young and Alison Shea, *Separating State from Church: A Research Guide to the Law of the Vatican City State* (99 *Law Library Journal* - 2007), https://scholarship.law.edu/cgi/viewcontent.cgi?article=1781&context=scholar; as occasionally updated at Alison Shea, *Updated: Separating State from Church: A Research Guide to the Law of the Vatican City State* (2012), retrieved March 9, 2018, http://www. nyulawglobal.org/globalex/Vatican1.html.
2. Synod of Bishops, *Justice in the World* (1971), 40.
3. United States Conference of Catholic Bishops; '*Socially Responsible Investment Guidelines*'; 2003; German Bishops Conference, '*Making Ethically-Sustainable Investments*'; *A guide for persons in financially responsible positions in Catholic institutions in Germany*; 2015. Conference of Bishops of France, 'Vade Mecum No. 3-2010; 2007.
4. Pope Francis, *Laudato Si'*, (2015), 129.
5. Pontifical Council for Justice and Peace, *Compendium of the Social Doctrine of the Church*, Libreria Editrice Vaticana, 2004.

Monsignor Romero:
Human Being, Christian
and Honourable Archbishop

JON SOBRINO SJ

I write from San Salvador where I lived for three years, from 1977 when Monsignor Romero was named archbishop until his murder in 1980. What I am going to say is known among us. Elsewhere, even if Monsignor is accepted and even admired, the approach to Monsignor can be and is often different. What I believe people like Ellacuría – also martyred –or this servant add is the direct and immediate personal experience of Monsignor. At his funeral mass Ellacuría said: 'In Monsignor Romero God passed through El Salvador.' He did not say it by virtue of his keen intelligence but of his actual contact with him. For my part, also by virtue of my contact with him, the first thing I wrote and said after his murder is that 'Monsignor Romero believed in God.'

What happened at the Vatican on the 14th of October, 2018 – his canonization – was important, but in the language of the ancestors it was *incidental*. The *substance* was Monsignor Romero himself, what he said and did, his total trust in God, his total obedience to God and his total dedication to the poor and victims of this world.

In El Salvador, on March 24, 1980, the day of his assassination, no one thought in terms of canonization, but many people spoke of the human, Christian, and archbishop excellence of Monsignor Romero. Crying, a peasant said: 'they have killed the saint'. A few days later Don Pedro Casaldáliga wrote: Saint Romero of America, our shepherd and martyr'.

It did not occur to anyone that one had to work in some curia to declare him a saint.

Not so on other occasions. When José María Escrivá de Balaguer died, many rushed to achieve his canonization. When Mother Teresa of Calcutta died, there was already great esteem for her virtues, especially for her loving partiality for those who suffer and are abandoned, and people hoped for her canonization. When Pope John Paul II died, one heard about the 'sudden saint.'

None of this occurred with the death of Monsignor Romero. And it is worth remembering that the day of the burial of the dead Romero, people lived the horrors that confronted the living Romero. In the cathedral square full of people, bombs exploded, many ran out to seek refuge, and left a mountain of hundreds of shoes. By the way, the official delegate of the Pope, Monsignor Corripio, asked to be taken to the airport immediately. On the other hand, there is a photo in which one can see six priests carrying on their shoulders the Monsignor's coffin, among them was Father Ignacio Ellacuría.

Let us address the substance. Monsignor Urioste used to repeat that Monsignor Romero was the most beloved Salvadoran, by the oppressed majority, and the most hated, by the oppressor minority.

What was the substance of October 14? A peasant was asked who Monsignor Romero was, and without hesitation, he answered: 'Monsignor Romero spoke the truth. He defended us, the poor. And for this, they killed him.' That is to say, he lived and died like Jesus of Nazareth.

I Monsignor Romero spoke the truth

He was a teller of the truth, he was possessed by it and spoke it with pathos. When reality was good for the poor, Monsignor told the truth as gospel, good news, with exultation and joy. When reality was bad, misery, oppression and repression, cruelty, death – especially for the poor-, Monsignor told the truth as bad news, with denunciation and unmasking, and he said it with pain. Filled with the truth, Monsignor was a beloved evangelist and an incorruptible prophet.

As 'truth teller', Monsignor Romero made judgments about reality, all of it. He let 'reality put in its word' (Karl Rahner), and he had the integrity to make public that word uttered by reality itself.

From these convictions Monsignor Romero spoke the truth in a form unknown in the country, before or after.

He spoke *vigorously*, referring to it as the most basic and fundamental: 'nothing is as important as human life, above all the life of the poor and oppressed' (March 16, 1980). In Puebla he asked Leonardo Boff: 'you, theologians, help us to defend the minimum that is the maximum given by God: life.'

He spoke *extensively*, in order to be able to tell 'all' the truth. That is why his Eucharistic celebrations on Sundays and in the cathedral could last an hour and a half or more.

He spoke *publicly*, 'from the rooftops' as Jesus requested, in the cathedral and through the radio station of the archbishopric YSAX, which was blown up and interfered with several times. His last homily had to be delivered by telephone connected to a station in Costa Rica. YSAX is still on the air, but without Monsignor, it has lost the exceptional value it had.

Monsignor spoke the truth *popularly*, learning many things from the people, so that, without knowing it, the poor and the peasants were co-authors in part of his homilies and pastoral letters. 'You and I have written the fourth pastoral letter' (August 6, 1979). 'Between you and I we make this homily' (September 16, 1979). And he made remarkable statements about his relationship with the people to tell the truth. 'I feel that the people are my prophet' (July 8, 1979). 'We made such a deep reflection that I believe that the bishop always has much to learn from his people' (September 9, 1979)

And he was also popular because Monsignor respected and appreciated 'reason', the course of the people, of simple people. And he successfully avoided taking steps toward religious infantilization, a danger that is usually normal in the pastoral realm.

II He defended us, the poor

In Latin America, and certainly in El Salvador, I believe that a good number of people accept the 'option for the poor'. We can say that it already belongs to ecclesiastical orthodoxy, with the danger of all orthodoxy of filing down the edges and diluting the essentials. Without underestimating the good things said at Puebla about poverty and the poor, especially the startling litany of the faces of the poor (p. 32-39), their multitude (p.

29), their structural causes and their demands (p. 30), I insist on a more precise understanding of the option, than what appears in the theological formulation Puebla makes. It says in p. 1142:

> The poor merit preferential attention, whatever may be the moral or personal situation in which they find themselves. Made in the image and likeness of God, to be his children, this image is dimmed and even defiled. That is why God takes their defence and loves them.'

The peasant understood well the option for the poor of Monsignor Romero. 'He defended us, the poor.' I have nothing to add to this solemn sentence of the peasant. Nor the language he used: He defended us 'the poor', that is to say to us 'that we are poor'. The conclusion is that Monsignor defended the poor and oppressed of the country, not only loved them. Week after week, he defended the poor and victims with the truth that he proclaimed publicly in his homilies. He promoted popular organization and Legal Aid to defend peasants and victims. When the repression intensified, he opened the doors of the central seminary San José de la Montaña to welcome the peasants fleeing from Chalatenango – which certainly displeased several bishops.

It is clear that Monsignor defended the oppressed. But one also has to be clear on what it means to defend. To defend supposes confronting and, when necessary, struggling in the most human way possible against those who attack, impoverish, persecute, oppress and repress. By defending the poor, Monsignor faced those who lie and kill, whether they were people, institutions, or structures. And his was a primordial defence, which went beyond what is conventionally understood as 'defending a case' with the purpose, in addition, of 'winning a case'. He worked and struggled to win the battered reality, justice and the truth. More deeply, he worked and struggled so that sometimes they would not lose the ones usually lost.

Let us look at a remarkable confrontation. The Supreme Court of Justice had publicly summoned him to say the names of the 'judges who sold themselves', who Monsignor had denounced in his Sunday homily. Monsignor's advisors were frightened, and they did not know how Monsignor would come out well from such a summons. Monsignor did not change. In his next homily, he made it clear in the first place that he had not said 'judges who sell themselves', but 'venal judges'. But he did not linger on whether he said or did not say this or that, which did not matter, but without further ceremony he went to the heart of the matter.

What is the Supreme Court of Justice doing? Where is the transcendental role in a democracy of this power that should be above all powers and claim justice to everyone who tramples it? I believe that a great part of the malaise of our country has its main key here, in the president and all of the collaborators of the Supreme Court of Justice, who with more integrity should demand from the chambers, the courts, the judges, all the administrators of this sacrosanct word, *justice*, that they are really *agents of justice*, (April 30, 1978)

Monsignor was the defender of the poor with all that he was and had. Five days before he was murdered, a foreign journalist asked him how it was possible, in such a difficult situation, to be in solidarity with the Salvadoran people, he replied: 'He who cannot do anything else, prays'. But do, do everything you can, he came to say. And he remembered the reason for that necessary doing. 'Do not forget that we are men [...] and that here they are suffering, dying, fleeing, taking refuge in the mountains'. At the University of Louvain he had said 'the glory of God is that the poor live'. To defend the poor is to defend God.

III And for this he was killed

The peasant got it right. In the biblical tradition 'telling the truth' is an imperative that comes from afar. And from afar comes also how dangerous the sphere is in which the truth moves. 'The evil one is a murderer and a liar', says the Gospel of John (8:44). First he brings death, and then he conceals it.

Monsignor was surrounded by death and the dead, and very recently by murdered priests on which we are now going to focus. During his life six priests were killed. And from the first murder to that of the Jesuits of the UCA in 1989, the number rose to 18. In Guatemala something similar happened.

Monsignor spoke a lot about the murder of priests, not considering them more important than other murders, and in fact he always scrupulously remembered everyone, laypeople, who had been murdered. But because of their ecclesial, and often Christian, symbolism, he spoke and reflected more strongly when the murdered person was a priest. 'I have to go to collect corpses', he began his homily on June 19, 1977 in Aguilares, referring to the murder of Father Grande and his two companions. Monsignor understood very soon that 'collecting corpses' was going to be an essential element of his archbishop's ministry.

In 1979, another three priests were killed (Octavio Ortiz, Rafael Palacios and Alirio Macías). Monsignor delved into the reality of these murders and concluded with blunt words: 'whoever gets in the way is killed' (23rd September). He kept them explicitly present: I want to remember with affection and be in solidarity with the assassinated priests' (16th September). In scandalous words he proclaimed the ecclesial importance of the murdered ones having been priests. 'It would be sad if in a country where people are killing so horrifically, priests did not also number among the victims. They are the testimony of a Church incarnate in the interests of the poor' (24th June). And one month later he said: 'I am happy, brothers, that our Church is being persecuted, precisely for its preferential option for the poor and for trying to be incarnate in the interest of the poor' (15th July).

He was aware of how difficult it was to fulfil what he said: 'how difficult it is to let oneself be killed for the love of the people' (12th August). But he remained firm: 'the shepherd does not want security until they give it to his flock' (22 July). He was consistent and increasingly radical until the end of his life:

As a pastor I am bound by divine mandate to give my life for those I love, who are all the Salvadorans, even those who are going to kill me… You can tell them, if they kill me, I forgive and bless those who do it. (March 1980).

I would not like to end without clarifying that Monsignor Romero was not killed simply for loving the truth – which usually occurs – but for speaking it.

This martyr-like attitude was fundamental from the beginning. On August 21, 1977, celebrating his birthday, he said in his homily: 'I have understood once again that my life does not belong to me but to you'.

Let us return to the 14th of October. That day, together with Monsignor Romero, they also canonized Pope Paul VI. I think they both appreciated each other. Monsignor was thankful for the *Evangelii Nuntiandi* of Paul IV and brought it to bear on his pastoral mission. And what struck him most about the pope happened on his trip to Rome. He went to talk with him shortly after the murder of Father Rutilio Grande. Paul VI, with great affection, gripped his hand and said, 'avanti, coragio'.

I end with the words of Ignacio Ellacuría, already cited: 'With Monsignor Romero, God passed through El Salvador'. They are the words of one martyr to another.

Translated by Thia Cooper

Contributors

PAUL DUMOUCHEL is professor at the Graduate School of Core Ethics and Frontier Sciences, Ritsumeikan University, Kyoto, Japan, where he teaches political philosophy and philosophy of science. He is the author of *Emotions* (Seuil, 1999), *The Ambivalence of Scarcity and Other Essays* and *The Barren Sacrifice* both at Michigan State University Press. With Reiko Gotoh he edited *Against Injustice: The New Economics of Amartya Sen* (Cambridge University Press, 2009) and *Social Bonds as Freedom* (Berghahn Books, 2015). His most recent book, with Luisa Damiano, is *Living With Robots* (Harvard University Press, 2017).

Address: Graduate School of Core Ethics and Frontier Sciences, Ritsumeikan University, 56-1 Toji-in Kitamachi, Kita-ku, Kyoto 603-8577 JAPAN
Email: dumouchp@ce.ritsumei.ac.jp

BENEDIKT PAUL GÖCKE is professor for the philosophy of religion and scientific theory in the Catholic Theological Faculty of the Ruhr-Universität Bochum. He is doing research into the philosophy of Karl Christian Friedrich Krause (1781-1832), on scientific theory and digital anthropology. He is the author of *The Panentheism of Karl Christian Friedrich Krause* (New York, 2018) and *A Theory of the Absolute* (Basingstoke, 2014). He is the editor of *Die Wissenschaftlichkeit der Theologie* (Münster 2018) and *After Physicalism* (Indianapolis, 2012). He has also published numerous articles in various specialist journals.

Address: Lehrstuhl für Religionsphilosophie und Wissenschaftstheorie, Katholisch-Theologische Fakultät, Ruhr-Universität Bochum, Universitätsstraße 150, 44801 Bochum, Germany
Email: Benedikt.goecke@rub.de

PAULO BENANTI is a Franciscan friar of the Third Order Regular. He graduated in ethics and theology at the Pontifical Gregorian University in Rome and pursued further study at Georgetown University in Washington DC, where he was able to do research into the world of biotechnologies. He currently teaches ethics of technologies, neuroethics, bio-ethics and moral theology at the Pontifical Gregorian University.

Address: Dipartimento di Teologia morale, Facoltà di Teologia, Pontificia Università Gregoriana, Piazza della Pilotta 4, 00187 Rome – Italy

Email: benanti@unigre.it

DOMINIK BURKARD is professor of Church history in the Middle Ages and Modern Times in Würzburg. His special research interests are: the history of science and the university, the Roman Inquisition and the Congregation for the Index, Church-State relations, Constitutional History of the Church, the Catholic Enlightenment, Catholicism in the 19th and 20th Centuries, Church and Theology under National Socialism

Address: Lehrstuhl für Kirchengeschichte des Mittelalters und der Neuzeit, Julius-Maximilians-Universität Würzburg, Sanderring 2, D-97070 Würzburg, Germany

Email: dominik.burkard@theologie.uni-wuerzburg.de

PETER KANYANDAGO is a priest from the Archdiocese of Mbarara, Uganda. He has worked in different capacities in Uganda Martyrs University from 1994-2016. He was Director of the project that led to the founding of the University of Saint Joseph Mbarara (USJM), the first private diocesan university in Uganda. He has researched into and published widely in theology, African and Development Studies.

Address: Professor of Ethics and Development Studies, Uganda Martyrs University, P. O. Box 5498, Kampala, Uganda

Email: pkanyandago@gmail.com

KURUVILLA PANDIKATTU SJ (born 1957) is a professor of Physics, Philosophy and Religion at Jnana Deepa Vidyapeeth, Pune, India. Currently, he is the Dean, Faculty of Philosophy, Jnana-Deepa Vidaypeeth,

Pune, India. He has been actively involved in dialogue between science and religion. He is a Jesuit priest belonging to Dumka-Raiganj Province of the Society of Jesus. Main topics of his research are: anthropology, eschatology, life-management and transhumanism.

Address: Faculty of Philosophy, Jnana-Deepa Vidyapeeth, Pune, India
Email: kuru@kuru.in or kuru@jdv.edu

SHARON A. BONG is Associate Professor in Gender and Religious Studies at the School of Arts and Social Sciences, Monash University Malaysia. She graduated with a Ph.D. in Religious Studies (2002) and M.A. in Women and Religion (1997), University of Lancaster, UK. She has authored *The Tension Between Women's Rights and Religions: The Case of Malaysia* (2006). She was the former coordinator of the Ecclesia of Women in Asia and a forum writer for the Catholic Theological Ethics in the World Church.

Address: School of Arts & Social Sciences, Building 2, Level 6, Room 13 (2-6-13), Monash University Malaysia, Jalan Lagoon Selatan, 47500 Bandar Sunway, Selangor, Malaysia
Email: Sharon.bong@monash.edu

JANINA LOH (née Sombetzki) works as a philosopher of technology at the university of Vienna on subjects such as the ethics of robotics, transhumanism and post-humanism, feminist philosophy of technology, responsibility, Hannah Arendt and ethics in the sciences.

Address: Universitätsassistentin im Bereich, Technik- und Medienphilosophie, Institut für Philosophie, Universität Wien, Universitätsstraße 7 (NIG), C 0326, 1010 Wien, Austria
Email: janina.loh@univie.ac.at

JACOB J. ERICKSON is Assistant Professor of Theological Ethics in the School of Religion at Trinity College Dublin, Ireland. His work attempts to evoke an ecotheology of planetary conviviality – the playful and just cherishing of life together – in the midst of current ecological crises, emerging perspectives in the wake of global warming, and new challenges in energy production. Erickson's writing meditates on the complex relationships of earth and divinity, contemporary environmental ethics and queer theory, classical Christian theologies and contemporary constructive theopoetics. With Marion Grau, he co-chairs the Sacred Texts, Theory, and Theological Construction Unit and serves on the Steering Committee for the Martin Luther and Global Lutheran Traditions Unit for the American Academy of Religion. Erickson is currently working on an extended project on the intersections of global warming and theology called *A Theopoetics of the Earth: Divinity in the Anthropocene*.

Address: School of Religion, Trinity College Dublin, Dublin 2, Republic of Ireland

Email: ericksoj@tcd.ie

ENRICO GALAVOTTI Born in Mirandola (MO) in 1971, he studied at the University of Bolo-gna and in 2002 earned a degree in the specialisation of Religious Studies at Bologna's Alta Scuola Europea di Scienze Religiose. He has taught at the University of Bologna and Modena-Reggio Emi-lia. He is currently Associate Professor of History at the 'Gabriele d'Annunzio' University of Chieti-Pescara; he is a member of the Bologna Fondazione per le scienze religiose and of the inter-national board of editors for 'Concilium'. Publications include: *Il professorino. Giuseppe Dossetti tra crisi del fascismo e costruzione della democrazia* (Il Mulino, Bologna 2013) and *Il pane e la pace. L'episcopato di Loris Francesco Capovilla in terra d'Abruzzo* (Textus, Pescara 2015).

Address: Università degli Studi 'G. d'Annunzio' di Chieti-Pescara, Dipartimento di Lettere, Arti e Scienze Sociali, Campus Universitario – Via dei Vestini, 39 - I-66100 CHIETI SCALO

Email: enrico.galavotti@unich.it

LEONARDO PARIS lay theologian, born in Trento in 1977. He earned a Licence and Doctorate in Theology from the Pontifical Gregorian University and a degree in Clinical and Community Psychology from's 'La Sapienza' University. He is permanent lecturer in Dogmatic Theology at Trento's 'Romano Guardini' Higher Institute of Religious Studies and lecturer in charge at Bolzano's Institute of Religious Studies and at Padua's Triveneto Faculty of Theology. Publications include: *Sulla libertà. Prospettive di teologia trinitaria tra neuroscienze e filosofia*, Città Nuova, Rome 2012; *Teologia e neuroscienze. Una sfida possibile*, Queriniana, Brescia 2017.

Address: Istituto Superiore di Scienze Religiose 'Romano Guardini',
Corso 3 Novembre 46, I - 38122 Trento
  Email: l.paris@diocesitn.it

SÉAMUS P. FINN OMI is responsible for the Faith Consistent Investing
program for the Oblate Investment Pastoral Trust www.oiptrust.org. He
is also Director of the Justice/Peace and Integrity of Creation Ministry of
the Missionary Oblates of Mary Immaculate. Rev. Finn has represented
the Oblates at the Interfaith Center on Corporate Responsibility www.iccr.
org in New York since 1988 and currently serves as the ICCR board chair.
  Address: 391 Michigan Ave, Washington DC 20017
  Email: seamus@omiusa.org

JON SOBRINO was born in 1938 in Barcelona to a Basque family and
completed his studies in Spain, Germany and the USA. A Jesuit in the
Central American province since 1957, he has been living in El Salvador
since 1974. He is a professor of theology and director of the 'Monsignor
Romero' Center at the Catholic University of Central America based in
San Salvador. He is a member of the international leadership committee of
Concilium. His publications include: *Cristología desde América Latina*,
México, 1976; *Monseñor Romero*, San Salvadorm 1989; *Jesucristo
liberador. Lectura histórico-teológica de Jesús de Nazaret*, San Salvador,
1991; *El principio misericordia*, Santander, 1992; *La fe en Jesucristo.
Ensayo desde las víctimas*, Madrid, 1999, 2000; *Cartas a Ellacuría*,
Madrid – San Salvador, 2004; *Fuera de los pobres no hay salvación.
Pequeños ensayos utópico-proféticos*, Madrid, 2007. He wrote with
Ignacio Ellacuría, murdered in 1993, the work *Mysterium Liberationis. I
concetti fondamentali della teologia della liberazione*, Borla – Cittadella,
Roma – Assisi, 1992.
  Address: Universidad Centroamericana José Simeón Cañas, Apartado
Postal (01) 168, Final Boulevard Los Próceres, San Salvador, El Salvador.
  Email: jsobrino@cmr.uca.edu.sv

CONCILIUM
International Journal of Theology

FOUNDERS
Anton van den Boogaard; Paul Brand; Yves Congar, OP; Hans Küng;
Johann Baptist Metz; Karl Rahner, SJ; Edward Schillebeeckx

BOARD OF DIRECTORS
President: Thierry-Marie Courau OP
Vice-Presidents: Susan Abraham, Linda Hogan, Stefanie Knauss,
Carlos Mendoza-Álvarez OP, Daniel Franklin Pilario CM

BOARD OF EDITORS
Susan Abraham, Los Angeles (USA)
Michel Andraos, Chicago (USA)
Mile Babić OFM, Sarajevo (Bosna i Hercegovina)
Antony John Baptist, Bangalore (India)
Michelle Becka, Würzburg (Deutschland)
Sharon A. Bong, Selangor (Malaysia)
Bernadeth Caero Bustillos, Cochabamba (Bolivia)
Stan Chu Ilo, Chicago (USA)
Catherine Cornille, Boston (USA)
Thierry-Marie Courau OP, Paris (France)
Geraldo Luiz De Mori SJ, Belo Horizonte (Brasil)
Margareta Gruber OSF, Vallendar (Deutschland)
Linda Hogan, Dublin (Ireland)
Huang Po-Ho, Tainan (Taiwan)
Stefanie Knauss, Villanova (USA)
Carlos Mendoza-Álvarez OP, Ciudad de México (México)
Esther Mombo, Nairobi (Kenya)
Gianluca Montaldi FN, Brescia (Italia)
Daniel Franklin Pilario CM, Quezon City (Filipinas)
João J. Vila-Chã SJ, Rome (Italia)

PUBLISHERS
SCM Press (London, UK)
Matthias-Grünewald Verlag (Ostfildern, Germany)
Editrice Queriniana (Brescia, Italy)
Editorial Verbo Divino (Estella, Spain)
EditoraVozes (Petropolis, Brazil)

Concilium Secretariat:
Couvent de l'Annonciation
222 rue du Faubourg Saint-Honoré
75008 – Paris (France)
secretariat.concilium@gmail.com
Executive secretary: Gianluca Montaldi FN

www.concilium.in

HYMNS
Ancient & Modern

The Canterbury Dictionary of HYMNOLOGY

The result of over ten years of research by an international team of editors, The Canterbury Dictionary of Hymnology is the major online reference work on hymns, hymn-writers and traditions.

www.hymnology.co.uk

CHURCH TIMES

The Church Times, founded in 1863, has become the world's leading Anglican newspaper. It offers professional reporting of UK and international church news, in-depth features on faith, arts and culture, wide-ranging comment and all the latest clergy jobs. Available in print and online.

www.churchtimes.co.uk

Crucible

Crucible is the Christian journal of social ethics. It is produced quarterly, pulling together some of the best practitioners, thinkers, and theologians in the field. Each issue reflects theologically on a key theme of political, social, cultural, or environmental significance.

www.cruciblejournal.co.uk

JLS

Joint Liturgical Studies offers a valuable contribution to the study of liturgy. Each issue considers a particular aspect of liturgical development, such as the origins of the Roman rite, Anglican Orders, welcoming the Baptised, and Anglican Missals.

www.jointliturgicalstudies.co.uk

magnet

Magnet is a resource magazine published three times a year. Packed with ideas for worship, inspiring artwork and stories of faith and justice from around the world.

www.ourmagnet.co.uk

For more information on these publications visit the websites listed above or contact **Hymns Ancient & Modern:**
Tel.: +44 (0)1603 785 910
Write to: Subscriptions, Hymns Ancient & Modern,
13a Hellesdon Park Road, Norwich NR6 5DR

Concilium Subscription Information

October	**2019/4:** *Christianities and Indigenous Peoples*
December	**2019/5:** *Queer Theologies: Becoming the Queer Body of Christ*
February	**2020/1:** *Contextual Theologies Facing the Challenge of Global Violence*
April	**2020/2:** *Masculinities*
July	**2020/3:** *Theology, Power and Governance*

New subscribers: to receive the next five issues of Concilium please copy this form, complete it in block capitals and send it with your payment to the address below. Alternatively subscribe online at www.conciliumjournal.co.uk

Please enter my annual subscription for Concilium starting with issue 2019/2.

Individuals
_____ £52 UK
_____ £75 overseas and (Euro €92, US $110)

Institutions
_____ £75 UK
_____ £95 overseas and (Euro €120, US $145)

Postage included – airmail for overseas subscribers

Payment Details:
Payment can be made by cheque or credit card.
a. I enclose a cheque for £/$/€ _____ Payable to Hymns Ancient and Modern Ltd
b. To pay by Visa/Mastercard please contact us on +44(0)1603 785911 or go to www.conciliumjournal.co.uk

Contact Details:
Name ....
Address ....
....
Telephone .... E-mail ....

Send your order to *Concilium,* **Hymns Ancient and Modern Ltd**
13a Hellesdon Park Road, Norwich NR6 5DR, UK
E-mail: concilium@hymnsam.co.uk
or order online at www.conciliumjournal.co.uk

Customer service information
All orders must be prepaid. Your subscription will begin with the next issue of Concilium. If you have any queries or require Information about other payment methods, please contact our Customer Services department.